Pandemic Puzzle Poems

Selected by
Diane Frank and Prartho Sereno

BLUE LIGHT PRESS ◆ 1ST WORLD PUBLISHING

1st WORLD
PUBLISHING

SAN FRANCISCO ◆ FAIRFIELD ◆ DELHI

BLUE LIGHT PRESS
www.bluelightpress.com
Email: bluelightpress@aol.com

Selected by Diane Frank and Prartho Sereno

Cover painting:
"Morning Poems" by Prartho Sereno

Book and Cover Design:
Melanie Gendron
www.melaniegendron.com
Email: gentarot@comcast.net

Library of Congress Cataloging-in-Publication Data

ISBN: 978-1-4218-3708-6

Pandemic Puzzle Poems

Contents

Introduction

This book is a gathering of community. It chronicles our Pandemic Times through the eyes, hearts, and minds of poets. Along with the lockdown of many aspects of our society, it has been a time of tremendous social unrest. Everyone had to find their own ways of coping. The pandemic took away many things – a bevy of customary comforts, celebrations, and enlivenments. But it also gave. One of its most radical gifts was time. Another – ourselves. Every morning during lockdown, a shiny new satchel of 24 hours was delivered to our door, to be spent, for the most part, with ourselves.

Strange, isn't it, how in our interminable frenzied race, no matter how fast we ran, we were always short on time? And how now, suddenly, a great majority of us had more than we knew what to do with – a world of time for getting to know the one we'd always hoped to make a deeper connection with: that quizzical one in the mirror.

Not that it was easy. Especially in the beginning, it was incredibly difficult to be stripped of the comforts and challenges of gathering and other delightful and not-so-delightful distractions. But slowly, many of us began to see this inward turning as precisely what had been missing. As we gave ourselves over to the simplest things – baking bread, cleaning out long-neglected drawers, sending off handwritten letters, unearthing those boxes of jigsaw puzzles from the back of the cupboard – the muses in us awakened and began to speak.

Between our puzzlings over the jig-sawed pieces and the scattered bits of our lives, art arrived. For the poets in this book, the art came flying in the form of new poems. We began to sense that perhaps there had been some curious wisdom in setting up the card table and spilling out the myriad jig-sawed contents from the puzzle box. The quest to bring all the pieces into a meaningful whole became a kind of Zen koan – a powerful riddle with the potential of shifting our entire way of seeing.

As we worked at them, the puzzles taught us things. When you first look at the scramble of parts spread across a table, all the pieces look pretty much alike. But it turns out that each piece is so utterly unique that there is only one place for it in the entire world of that puzzle. Without it, there is an unhappy gap, a black hole, a picture that is sadly incomplete.

The idea for this book began with Pandemic Puzzle Poems. Last spring, several poets in the Blue Light Press community wrote poems about doing jigsaw puzzles during the lockdown. A favorite, by Michelle Demers, is in the shape of a jigsaw puzzle. We thought it would be a great idea to do a chapbook, but as you can see, the book expanded to include all aspects of the pandemic times – how we feel during these most unusual times, how we are coping, how we are spending our time, what has changed in our lives, and how to stay inspired during the quiet time.

When George Floyd was murdered, the scope of the book expanded again. Poets stepped into the role of speaking as the conscience of our society, calling for social justice. We were flooded with poems to grieve George Floyd and others who were harmed, poems about the protests, and calls for change. One of the poets in this book lives in Minneapolis, across the alley from the club where George Floyd worked as a security guard. Another layer of poems came in during the terrible fires in California and the West Coast.

We rediscovered, as always, the poems that move us most are the ones that come from deep inside. To complete the book, we asked for positive visions about the future and how we can create it. We also asked for inspiring poems about the joy and mystery of being alive. Poetry reminds us what it means to be human.

We hope that some of what you read here will help you find meaning from your own Pandemic Times, and as things open up again, the reawakening of the world with a new vision of what it means to be human.

Love and Blessings,
Diane Frank,
     Chief Editor, Blue Light Press
Prartho Sereno,
     Fourth Poet Laureate of Marin County, California

Pandemic Diaries: Fragments of Resistance

NoNoNoNoNoNoNoNoNoNoNoNoNoNoNoNoNoNoNo
No   going out   No
No   touching your face   No
No   No
No   shopping in stores   No
No school in classrooms   No
No   No
No   No
No   kissing hugging   No
No   No
No eating in restaurants   No
No lingering in grocery stores   No
No browsing in bookshops   No
No long trips in cars, buses, trains, planes   No
No spectator sports   No
No   No
No   symphonies   concerts   No
No   haircuts   No
No money   tips   paycheck   job   No
No food   toilet paper   No
No saying goodbye   graduation   prom   picnics   No
No   No
No peace till it's over   No
NoNoNoNoNoNoNoNoNoNoNoNoNoNoNoNoNoNoNo

On the Rise

It's just a flight of cream-colored roses
that seems to cup the last of daylight
to charm and soothe this little house,
while twilight gradually anchors trees and shrubbery
all around. But it feels like more.

Down at the street, runners pass the gates
into the cemetery's dead-end turnaround.
None of them dressed for an occasion;
just a summer trot-by, in shorts and tank tops;
and all of them unreckoning,
in a plane of possible contagion.

Walkers and cyclists too eat up the asphalt
in rhythmic procession. Mostly they are masked
against infection by the virus, by the century,
by squabbling in the capitol, the wholesale loss
of civility and comity and compassion.

The barefaced hold their breath, pull up
the strained necks of their tees,
defer to hope and longing. Worldwide,
how many succumbed to the virus today?
Everywhere the numbers catching fire.

Seen from this remove (my domestic haven),
the roses seem to fly at sundown,
as a dancer alone onstage
might toy with gravity
under the outpouring
of love's unstated presence.

Normal

Viruses are themselves an enigma that exist on the edges of life.
– from The Great Influenza by John M. Barry

It's true: *Invisible enemies are worst.*
Memories may shift, but who believes
the wisteria in the park, for instance, might be
aware of microbes mowing down mankind?
The vine can't think; it's just a plant that bends
toward light, and lures in bugs for pollination,
now that winter's shadow has rolled away
and spring uncoils to sunny warmth and ease.
In normal times, we start to say, not wanting
to acknowledge our new norm: this universal
stalking-death that tenants us, hitchhiking
on our architecture like some sci-fi monster
hiding in the air ducts of an interstellar cruiser.

Viruses don't live, scientists counsel,
as if that news consoled. But humankind
didn't track the malady around the globe
till body counts took off. In times before,
grace of habit let us trust repetition:
no surprises – just *things as they are,*
a la Mr. Stevens's florid arabesques.

Doesn't that lost era gleam antique, from here;
the deadly Spanish flu seem almost quaint,
the First World War appear somehow *naif.*
Our herdy mind harks back to old-time problems,
and demurs: *We put all those to rest…* discounting
how the Reaper lay us waste. And now,
these much-lulled generations later,
we're still in debt to death's sub-zero smirk.

Tell that to the wisteria and its veil of murmurous bees.
Tell it to the afternoon with warblers tuning up
exquisite instruments in the underbrush,
the hush of this world's presence all around us,
when each stir of human breath
cries out for normal.

Washing

We are washing our hands. In front of a stone spigot. A faucet. A tin basin. A bucket. A sink. With soap. With a washcloth. With a rag. We are opening up the lattices of our fingers, we are washing our knuckles, our wrists, we are turning our hands over so we can see our palms – the creases, the line that a palmist would say is the fate line, the health line, the heart line, the life line that curls under the ball of the thumb, the marriage line a crinkle to one side, lines formed when were in our mother's belly – we are lathering, we are swabbing, we are wiping, we are hoping we are scrubbing away that tiny sphere with its spicules. We are singing *Happy Birthday* or *God Save the Queen*, we are looking for bubbles, we are looking for foam, we are looking under our fingernails, we are drawing the sack of loneliness over our heads, trying to breathe inside its coarse hood, and our hands look wrinkled and drained from being washed so often, we are rubbing our palms together the way villains rub their hands together in a movie to signify they're going to get more money.

Aunt Garnet

I. Spanish Flu 1918

This pandemic loved youth,
the twenty-somethings –
sick soldiers sent off to France
dying mid-ocean
not in the trenches
and the virginal, like you, Aunt Garnet,
your ruby name an amulet
against negative energy.

Who were you, Aunt,
purified by wind so strong
you could cut steel?
Is that why you went down
death's byways,
certain of your healing powers?
How is it contagion loved you
and not your sisters,
Lola and Grandmother Eva,
nor Dad, who was seven.
What truth failed you?
No one ever said
and I never asked.

Of the three sisters
I loved your name best,
girl of the cochineal
girl of firelight in Noah's ark,
girl of the heart chakra.

II. Covid 19, 2020

I look for you among Dad's photos,
celluloid ghost
quiet as a secret
flowing into willow shadow,
no oral history to sanctify your passing,
no notes unlocking your song.

But 90 years later you reappear
on Dad's last day on earth,
his eyes opening on mine
from his long slumber
when I enter his hospital room
and he coos his amen,
as if seeing Persephone
released from the underworld,
astonishing then, now omen,
"Ohhh, Garnet!"

Praise Song for What Is

Praise the frozen rain, the icicles daggering
the trees, the grey snow sludge. Praise
the shiver, the wet wind cutting through clothes,
the frozen water troughs. Blessed be
the hard frost, the frozen pond,
the apple tree sapling snapped in half.

Praise autumn and spring, the hot then cold
then hot again. Praise the corn mazes,
the haystacks, the reaping what we've sown.
Blessed be the fig tree, the honeycomb, the hive.
Praise the kudzu, the poison ivy,
the forsythia screaming yellow at a fence.

Praise the mosquito, the itch,
the scratch. Praise the heat waves
rising from asphalt, the stopped
highway traffic, and my a/c out.
Blessed be the dusty, the wilted, the dry
husks of corn in summer drought.

Praise the possum lumbering
into the chicken coop,
the fox slinking the wood's edge.
The owl, the hawk, blessed be
their swift descent.
Praise the failures, the losses. Blessed be
the broken path that brought me here.

One Last Drink

The horses in your chest
have no destination,
just the racetrack of your ribs.
Do not pray for dawn
or nighttime or even gin
to stop this running. Rather,
gallop in the field with your herd
until you come to the fence's edge.
We live in an in-between world.
This small faith of showing up
is not the moon's sister, is not
someone else's mouth opening,
but is your own seedling
in a dixie cup on the windowsill
above the kitchen sink.
Surely, religion is the trauma of thirst
in the desert of your life,
but do not go to a well. Water –
the water is everywhere, is everyone.
Turn on the faucet and drink.

Superstitions About Holding One's Breath

As long as you are breathing, there's more right with you
than there is wrong. – Jon Kabat-Zinn

You who have lost the trick of losing
yourself in the forest. You who have forgotten
the secrecy of fiddlehead ferns,
fox grapes, and oyster mushrooms.
You who have burned in endless fluorescence,
neon lights, and shot glasses. You who are
holding your breath
like you're living in a cemetery –
Come to the yard at night, with your flashlight
aimed into the tangle of grass,
see the eyeshine of dozens of wolf spiders.
Stand until there's a difference between staring,
being stared at, and seeing light.
Until you feel the difference between inhale,
exhale, everywhere in your body,
until the pauses between every breath
becomes a rest, a shining.

Compassion

While listening to Nessi Gomes sing "All Related"

It is all so big...
from blue ocean emerging
out of morning fog,
to hearts that re-open
after searing grief
closed them for a long time.

Here, I am among fragrant white
jasmine flowers and fledgling crows.
A sea breeze caresses my skin
like a lover whose touch
you have waited all your life
to feel. And bliss
comes a thousand simple ways...
tray of cookies lifted
from a hot oven, or lyrics sung
that lead you home to yourself.

This morning I gave five dollars
to a kid on the street
who said he was hungry.
Everyone else ignored him
so when the money passed
between our hands
the gratitude in his eyes
filled me and compassion
became the thread that connects
everything.

Devotion

Day 68 of Covid-19 sheltering in

My daughter's hands –
still small and slender
at age thirty-six,
fingers as graceful
as swaying meadow grass,
nails tapered to
crescent moon tips.

When she visits,
several times a week,
I hear her light step
on the deck stairs,
move chairs six feet apart
so we can safely sit together,
visit for a spell.

We raise our arms
over our heads in virtual hugs,
the way her baby brother
used to do as the school bus
carried him off to kindergarten.

Then I watch those lovely hands
carry each full shopping bag,
set it gently on the outdoor table,
full of groceries to sustain us
while we shelter in.

Night Before Women's March

Late night, sliver of moon –
wrapped in shadows I dream
I am holding the limp bodies of children
who died at the southern border.
I swaddle them in linen,
place them gently back into the arms
of their distraught parents...

...startled, I awaken
damp with sweat and tears,
recognize this wall of grief
is the same one I couldn't climb over
after my own son died.

How can I say I'm sorry?
Apologize for a nation that has
torn itself apart with disregard
for the sanctity of all lives?

Only five a.m. I rise up from bed,
put my hiking boots, pink hat and
What Would MLK do? sign by the front door.
Later when I leave for the march, I know
I will carry the weight of those children
along the streets of my hometown.

Breathing Room

I breathe today, automatic, slightly asthmatic,
my voice squeezes out breath, water vapor. Breath,
holding us alive, is slightly blue. Water molecules
absorb red on the color spectrum at atomic speed.

Who teaches color values on the human spectrum?
What color are you when revolving red lights
pull your vehicle over?

Are you so polite your mother would wonder at you,
and is your little stash well secure or didn't you know
your passenger had some, crossing into Florida,
headed back to school? Did you pull over
for a Texas officer to pass but failed to signal?
Were you pulled over in St. Paul for a fix-it ticket?
Did you head out for an early jog around Fenway Park
in your cold-morning hoodie, a knife in your sock and
keys between your fingers? Were you out for a drive
with friends? For a walk to buy some milk?

What color are you? Will your breath, weaponized,
choke out of you for a mistake or no reason?

Unlike breath, the sky is every rainbow color,
assembled yet scattered molecules, blue most of all.

Call it breathing room, a concept we relearn to live
together these plague days, even as skies radiate light,
even as someone's breath is stoppered on a highway or
familiar neighborhood.

And red? Lightwaves of red are longest, take longer
to reach us. Blood-red, passion-red, chances at life
finite in any ordinary month.
And blue – like a trace of shadow –
pulsing code red to reconnect.

What would I give

to say
I gave it my all?
Did I ever?
Was I mostly just minding
my itsy-bitsy business
when I could have been
planting sage for honeybees
native fire-defiant trees
gardening all the goods I'd ever need?

What would I give
to say
I had no part in it
when I gaze back someday
see the blue glow of my planet
gone soot gray?

Features of a Ruin

And now that we know,
we can't close our eyes –
a whitewashed sky,
a forest dense,
a life resigned.
Pipeline packed with roiling mud,
coal mines closing in, breath blocked, body bent.
Sinkholes, marshland, desert wind –
the earth rebels.
We choose half-truths,
flames sparking our speech,
hate glazing our tongues.
We chase a fading shade,
the sun disguised behind billows of gray.
We know. And now we wait.

Inside

Inside tawny dunes pale yellow-green
clumps of grass dance with a fierce ocean wind.
Snowy plovers group and fly above the water,
round back and hop on one foot, searching
for tiny crabs in the wet sand.
Above us, stars squiggle and bend
like heat waves on blacktop.

Sometimes the stars are inside us.
I see their light shining
from every cell of our bodies,
this light
that grants wishes for free.

These days, behind our masks,
beneath these orbs sprinkled through icy space,
we look out and wave,
we hear the children's muffled laughter
through fabric that cannot block the stars
that shine out from each.

Since the folding in of winter, the potatoes
have grown more than eyes
and the pomegranates have burst
on the small tree that grows
next to the scarlet runner beans,
dry as the white whale skull that beckoned us,
Come, touch and pray, give thanks.

Deep longing returns the birds calls of laughter
on the play structure.
Joyful vibrations from the children

lighten broken hearts with hope and healing.
And the beans hang on the trellis, crackled –
they remind me of the whalebones and
maybe we could plant them and
what would they grow?

How many sweet red seeds
would it take to measure the stars?
How many purple spotted beans
would have to grow to reach heaven?
How many people will you recognize by their eyes?
And how will you know
you're in the universe where you belong?
Will you know the Light?
Will you reach for her, and hold her hand?

Ten Days After His Murder

In Memory, George Floyd, a black man,
who was murdered by a white policeman.

The night is full of marching,
looting and light pollution.
Peter, my nephew, a brown skinned cop,
is abused – shouts from hate-filled faces.
In the only patch of black
where I finally sleep, sorrow
leaks into my dreaming brain.

I wake in icy sweat and hear
the shrieks of sirens.
Though hungry and exhausted,
Peter acts like a peace officer on Lake Street,
wondering if he'll make it home alive.

In my near suburb, the rasping *thrup-thrup*
of an army helicopter so low,
I fear it will drop through the roof on me.
It whirrs next door. Searchlights
from the 'copter bleach neighborhood lawns,
and shadows spread like blood.

An Ecstasy of Bees and Cicadas

As the sky darkens, bees' buzzing
is a wave of loose-stringed violas
that fades in the cicadas'
steam, ceaseless cymbals,
and quick-sifting rice.

In the fine-grained,
autumn night, give praise
for their symphonies.
Love your life.

California Fires

The sun
is late
this
orange
pigment
ashen
dark
September
morning
having
feverishly
first
risen
thousands
of miles
away
in
the black
coffee
sky
above
a
roadside
diner
parking
lot

The
Outer
Planets

The moving
shadows
of the
outer
planets
spill over
my tongue
My words
leaving
at the
very edge
of memory

What is
left to
forget
I ask
the
Crows
who have
come
in the faint
morning light
to watch my
paper wings
unfold
and my
writing eye
open
inside
each arriving
dying moment

Poem for the
Early Morning
Barking Dog

I have to admit
that I like
and sometimes
envy
the way
you
persuade
the sun
to rise
each day

I'll try to explain about the fear

and how it mirrors desire, walking through
one door then another, the moon's reflection
pressed against glass, the dryer's tumble
of twisted sheets, the dog asleep at my feet, a song
I almost remember moving the scent of night
jasmine through the air, the heart's journey
continuing without direction as the world tilts
into darkness, as the world tips back into light

To-do Lists

"…and afterwards the opposite of nostalgia
begins to make sense."
—Eric Gramalinda

They're what we made, what we believed
kept us safe, if only we could get everything
checked off and put in order, maybe then we
could take a break and watch the stars fall
through another summer, another moment
arriving just like that, minus any opinion –
maybe now that everything has changed
we won't wait to welcome in fear, invite
love over for dinner, embrace each mess, hold
hands, forgive up one side, down the other.

Summer in the City

For the first time since the pandemic,
I drive down Ellis Street in San Francisco,
past Glide Memorial in the Tenderloin –
faces, bodies
angular, soft
running, walking, sitting
splayed upon the sidewalk
zigzagging through cars
stopping traffic.
One man jumps on the hood
of a truck in front of me.

Long lines of despair.
Food alongside feces
on the sidewalk,
in the street.

I want to see them as people –
not as a hoard
or inmates of a boundaryless,
outdoor mental institution –
an emergency ward.

I can take one at a time,
like the must-have-been-schizophrenic guy
who recently stood in front of our house
blasting a hose in the middle of the night
flooding the basement.

When I peered down from the deck
and asked him to please leave, he said,
"I will, but first can you tell me your name?"

Then he spewed loud and angry words
I could not understand.
With wiry strength, he ran off
with our heavy hanging planters
into the night.

Or the woman who screamed
I'm gonna kill you bitch
while she ran after me
and hit me over the head.
Ambulance, police report, never to be found.

But here,
I feel outnumbered
as the souls rise up
out of summer dust
crying to be born.

Silver Linings

My pet Leo doesn't know
a killer virus has jumped oceans,
traversed land and sky,
and holds the world hostage,
an ever present threat.

He gifts me each day
a silver lining, dancing circles
like a circus dog,
thrilled that I am home.
I would like to be that unaware.

About Time

Quarantine Poem # 6

Our household clocks, come time for spring-forward,
fall-back, are not always reset room
to room, one left daylight, another standard

but what is time in these times, when
the world itself stalls, March, April,
interminable May? We are revisiting

old calendars, each flipped to a different
photo: Bubb's Creek that summer of the bears,
a fist full of gravel from Dog Lake, 1985.

Each a prompt return to where we want to be.
Every home should have such time machines
to make becoming possible. Becoming

that self not quite you, but the one
that's meant to be. Where is she –
forward or back? Ahead or behind?

Something keeps ticking on the wall,
hands go 'round.

Even the weather suspended, tossed back to us.
These old poplars flailing in the late May rain
waving, signaling.

A House to Fit the Future into

When it came, long expected as it was,
it was nothing as it should be: features misaligned,
dimensions proportional only to itself.

The light was indistinct, its outline
blurred against the sky.
I could not tell its shape.

We build houses in our imaginations –
walls and roof, complete – to fit the future into.
What poor architects we are shown to be

when it arrives as a tsunami and not a volcano,
as a pandemic not an earthquake. We are left
looking at one another across

a sudden chasm of amazement
as it moves through our narrow streets,
obscuring familiar landmarks.

In truth, whatever we expect never comes
as we fear it, as we want it.

"All in This Together"

Quarantine Poem # 4

I imagine us swimming, yes, all of us, in an immense indoor
pool, arms flailing, legs splashing, each in our lanes,
six feet apart, the room awash in undulating light.

Or perhaps at sea's edge, waist deep,
plunging in, the murky water chill, half-lit;
the horizon an indistinct haze as we swim out,

the water deepening, sun-strewn beach no longer in view,
wind and whitecaps rising. All water and the motion
of water; companions half-glimpsed shadows at our side.

So we swim, heads just above water,
we swim.

Puzzling

I'd like to board the striped hot air balloon
in our jigsaw. Suspended in a basket,
I'd hang with the two gentlemen in top hats,
flying above the puzzle's riotous vignettes.

A royal elephant, draped in purple carpets,
his rider in a red turban.
Behind the saddle, a miniature gold temple.
Aqua neon tetras float
through orange anemones.
White-robed devotees gather at the Taj Mahal.
A geisha in a wooden rowboat dips fingers
into ripples on a lake.
Giraffes wade on padded leather hooves in Hokusai's Wave.

Puzzle loving guests
explore our constant jigsaws.
Gathered on the window bench, they lose themselves
in vibrant, odd shaped cardboard tiles.

Three thousand shapes locked together
like a mob of madcap spooning bedfellows,
done in months of loving dedication
before the plague set in.

Two thousand not yet placed,
waiting since mid-March
in a loveless heap across the table.
Touch is dangerous, unfinished.
Fragments, happy scene abandoned,
stuck in this too long interlude of isolation.

My Mother's Earrings

In the light from the window, the purple asters
on the kitchen table remind me of jewels,
something my mother would wear on her earlobes.
Bright greens and blues, muted pinks and purples
matching whatever outfit she was wearing.

Even toward the end, when all she wore were colorless
gowns that tied in the back, doing her best
to maintain her dignity in that sterile room
with nurses gossiping, my mother rose above it all,
elegant earrings shimmering
even as she was losing her own light.

The Year of Wasps

In August the wasps came,
three or four at a time on the smooth glass
of the bathroom window. Hard to tell
if they had just come in or were trying to get out.
They were easy to swat
and not aggressive, just fell to the sill,
resigned to their fate.

This was before the fires,
before a blanket of smoke
caused the exterminators to cancel
so we kept swatting.
Now we are down to one in four days.

Any other year we wouldn't have had the patience
but long days of isolation had us trained.
And the masks have come in handy with the smoke.

This morning, a long arm of sun
through the bathroom window,
the first birdsong in a week.
A faint buzz from the retreating wasps.

Pandemic Wander

Inside me is a long lean body,
inside me is a doughy round woman.
Near and around me
every thought I've ever had.
Lately I watch baking shows over and over
the same bakes by the same British bakers.
They want to win ferociously yet
they are kind to one another over and over again.

Walking I think
it's no joke we really do die.
I keep learning it over and over.
Falling back into wishful naïveté again and again.
The world is good, people are kind, and everything will be all right.
But then I see not all will be right,
some will be terribly wrong and some will say
"it is what it is".
We exist in a terrible mystery, a terrible lie.

After walking 10,000 steps over and over
following the curved route
up the staircases hidden between houses
next the steep streets with no sidewalks
and finally straight down the hill to home,
I hear someone's wind chimes just as I glance
at some bluebells and, of course,
it seems the flowers are ringing.

Almost home and I think
these are the fairytales we feel even now
when we know it is the time of the big bad wolf
or worse.

In the time of Covid 19

Praise the devil in the details.
The long walk on the very short pier.
Praise the underwater experience.
Praise holding your breath
long enough to know the surface
is yet to come.
Praise the entire planet
ball in space,
a curve ball thrown by no one knows
who.
Praise the throbbing night,
the blistering sun, the moonlight kiss,
the dawn.
Praise the awakening –
the time has come.
Praise the body
this one chance for air on skin.
Praise the almighty
the absolute
the one and only
and that first time you
called my name.
Praise the babe in arms.
Praise the final gaze.
Praise us from first to last.
We didn't know any better –
we just couldn't believe we were the angels
we were waiting for.

Auricular

I found a tiny cathedral fashioned from metal,
so small I had it installed in my left ear.
Though it's better than ear bud or hearing aid,
I tune out the sermons and homilies, the prayers
that have no prayer of getting there, the hopeful
couples promising forever, the squall
of an infant being christened, the tear-stricken
praise for a partner who has departed.

I only want to lean back in my lounger
and groove on the choral glories
of Mozart and Fauré and Arvo Pärt –
wavelengths that both haunt and soothe,
unlike the inane pronouncements
of President Orange Cockatoo,
who ignores the dire reports of the saints,
the masked and weary working the ER and the ICU.

But if you can't afford your own
Notre Dame or Hagia Sophia or Cologne,
you might try a virtual tour of the world's
submerged churches, where fearless fish slip
in and out like tourists, and no death toll
is spiking out of control, and dangerous
Narcissus, drowned in his own reflection,
can't make a sound.

In a Silent Way

I have nothing new to say about the moon.
And the best I can do about the heart
is in the picture window across the street:
a thin, changing outline of light – from winter blue
to lemon yellow to spring green to amethyst,
a slow-throb valentine to the night.
I won't say what darkness it dispels,
or at least resists, what menace
has just paid a visit, or is about to.
No need to be so time-specific. Time
has a way of recycling its dreadful
greatest hits, even as we're dead set
against them. When it comes to phases,
the moon knows enough to show, not tell,
a more reliable narrator than I'll ever be.
It says no darkness is absolute. Tonight
seems to agree, warm enough I can savor
a dark beer on the stoop. And the changing heart
is right here, watching for its old brother
to rise again, tireless in his brilliance.
One beacon in the dark, signaling to another.

"Our true blood: words"

– Francis Ponge

Sometime ago
a conspiracy took shape
light broke down

rain hid where it could
the camellia leaves
scattered slowly underground

the new alphabet was born
speech awoke
and we saw a way out

song – cure for the
mutilation of
small worlds

antidote to the stratagems
the blindness
of wrecked and abandoned tongues

Breath

The subject of your life and of the world is secret
you may decide now's the time to fly away

but you have learned that each day of living
grows deeper into the next

and the dreams you summon will consume your breath

this is our life   the heart will live until
it cannot see past the darkness

then breath will know it is time to summon light

where it first was born   for that final sound

       of your embrace

From *Zonal*

"What of writing itself as a passion?" – Geoffrey Hartman

1.

Photo of a hand, shadowed by a hand.
Inside the eye of a fly, worlds and breaches

of security: how we've come to witness
quieter still, slow awakening of spring,
outside of history's grasp or need to show.

What grows and what burns is design.
You will lose your way in liminal drifts:
Amid the signs and warnings,
Indecipherable forms/systems disabled

in the reaching and the grasping.
Have you come to notice fog's
conspiracy? Is there method
in your breathing? Time to grow
wings and set out for the obvious.

4.

When worlds collide choose stillness, choose
green's waning days, or footprints in the mud;

choose a planet such as ours, whose carbon holds
an engine of rebirth. For those awaiting signs, like
the recluse in his hut awaiting God, no more

wrong than the fisherman with his slack,
dark line awaiting silverfish on Oakland's pier.
Under sea's repose, a slowness and a speed.
The bleached-out coral knows a crime. When smallest

mouths are open, it's nativity or war. The skirmish
never ends. Nothing restive but our minds awaiting
legibility. You too will stumble into simplifying by degree,
grow lazy with solutions on a breezy night when truth
gives way to forces of desire. Know this too is measuring.

6.

Time speeded up is comedy – and time slowed down
its opposite. To know the ending is right is a nod

to convenience. What can sympathy mean when children
die at sea and parents weep and shake a fist?
There is a border crisis, where borders don't exist

any more than perfect love or painless birth.
The harms accumulate, until you gather
a lifetime of torn cloth. On the loom she knew
the truth, as white and black combined their powers.

The death of the artist, the death
of the critic, the death of the language. The last
speakers, two sisters who wouldn't speak to
one another. The tragi-comic gods own all the real
estate and in the end the blackness too.

8.

Riding this same subway/ planet Earth/
a young woman/ (dressed only in a Hefty bag)/

had trained her eyes on me/ Now nurses wear the same
to treat the ill, whose last words won't be heard
by loving ears. Cue the narrative, friends:

dystopia now (I watch a documentary about the painter
whose work I'd seen that year: how she had continued/
her disease slower/than our current plague/
her paintings large/ and glistening with life/:

"I can't believe I have to leave this world!")
But must we trade economy for love?
When worlds mourn at a distance, nothing
to hold except our worry beads and lists of needs:
from Lysol to goodbyes / deliver us, we pray/

12.

But who is speaking now, and how to Zoom the edges of the text?
Can meaning take its storied place on suddenly vacant shores?

The middle goes missing from the plot of how we train our minds to
        follow
all but tragedy, mortality pressed behind the ropes of well-earned fears.
While we try light and bleach and llama's blood to seek a cure,

history shifts its weight. We pass markers for the losses we endure,
whole Viet Nams of endings, cities falling ill, as fruit begins to form
in winter's face, and seasons pass in reference to our moons.
April 15 lilacs bloom, the flower moon is pink and low in what

we call a firmament of words and signs. We choose to read and "voice"
our fears though legibility encounters bewilderment, makes
sense of time outside of time, experience upended, the week coyotes
take LA, flamingos claim Mumbai, and monkeys loot Nepali shrines:
how the millions missing from the tale agree to disappear.

Neighborhood Watch

it's this morning
that matters
more than the matters
we are mourning

these masks that we wear
on top of the masks we have been wearing
since 2010
since 1910
since you asked about that apple
ever since that day you realized
there was a price to pay
for showing who you are

we are each other
and not in a campaign ad
or self help kind of way
we are each other
in a terrifying and liberating way
in a way that surgically removes
the comfort of the blanket
you thought was keeping you warm
in a way that makes every picture you take
a selfie

no one wants to see themselves
and they definitely don't want to see themselves
in someone else
not now
not then
we don't want it but we need it

it used to be we stoned you for saying these kind of things
until we realized no press is bad press
now we just blow up your timeline
and feed you to the bots
we don't undermine you
we undermine your message
we call you by the names that were handed out at the beginning
of class
to wear on your sleeve for the rest of your life
hedge fund manager
homeless architect
housewife
snowflake
fascist
we make sure we are on the same team as our parents
and their parents
we have our playbook
and know when to pull the cord
we mow the edges of our lawn
until they are sharp enough to cut

we arm ourselves with whatever we think
will protect us from the truth
we build our walls
high enough that they won't realize we're even there
high enough
that we will never escape

and when we are sure we've sealed every breach
we gaze into the void of our screens and mirrors
trying not to look at the reflection
trying not to notice we haven't locked anyone out
trying not to realize we've trapped the whole world in our home
quarantined now
with the whole universe
in the roofs of our mouths

Recount

I have not counted flicks of a tail of the mourning dove
each one must mean something – ready, willing, able.
Counting orders, controls, signifies. Wins. Heightened emotion
renders increased heartbeats – 140-150. I'll pay closer attention
to just what is worthy of counting. Not breaths, not blinks of an eye.
Seconds with my sister, calls I don't make. Wishes.
Human beings who died today at the hands of virulence. Violence.
Stop the fucking counting. Go quietly to the beach,
there are how many where you live? Fall on your knees on the sand,
countless grains, cry. I'll ask for something that resembles forgiveness.
Years til we know what in God's name we are doing.
Burrow in billions of numbers. Burrow deep in a garden,
a spirit, a body, a breath.

Ode to the Brave

They say
writing odes
is praise and nod
seeing splendid
in the plain, simple
so look,
golden acts
of everyday
clean hospital rooms
green curtains
sliding on a stainless track
gloved hands
blue with bravery
dexterity
in latex
covered.
This is not
your usual everydayness
it is early
rising
nurses, driving in the dark
shooting stars above –
doctors, it is you
and you
and you
over there
at a desk
scribbling words
into grand speeches
the Senate might hear.
Small gestures
light a candle
pray.

Say their names,
souls slipped in
the envelope of sunset.
There are too many
so, beloved
utter their names.
Sing. Chant.
Make them known.

Ode to My Smartphone

Whole cities inside you
complete with sparks
descending from fireworks
stories of migrants
trapped children, starvation
gorillas and leopards
swing, leap
rearing their proud heads
an elephant rider
a rodeo cowboy are all there
you light up your screen
tell me of families – jobless
and their gardens still grow
children show us
and the writers write
in the *Times* and the *Post*
make strange sense
of insanity
I ask you questions
about chicken and rice
how long, how much
what is the distance?
You keep up
in a tart British accent
"I don't respond to anger"
when my rant hurtled out
you scolded.
Don't connect
bad zone
bad phone
I have not learned
to train you

I say names of the dead
on your To Do List
you answer *they are not
in your contacts.*
Teach me to say
dance with me in Italian
a zillion shops lure
us in day & night
friends, unfriends
meditators sit with me
around the world
Norway, Africa, Belize
in my bedroom,
all close their eyes
you pray and ring bells.

Renaming COVID-19

I dislike the name COVID-19.
It's too technical and abstract.
How about pangolin plague
or badass bat bug
since pangolins and bats
carry similar strains? I want
to see the face of a villain:
scales and a snout, or red eyes
and razor-sharp teeth.

Or how about serpent syndrome,
to be more biblical;
the corona curse, suggesting
power and evil; or Earth scourge
to bring in geography
without offending anyone?
Admitting politics, both
domestic and international,
we could call it fiasco fever.

It needs a name that evokes
science fiction, Armageddon,
a dystopian nightmare.
COVID-19 sounds like
it could be a new medication
or maybe a new planet,
one where we could go outside
without fear and even touch
each other, which, of course,
is just what we need.

Pandemic Dream

I was on vacation in a foreign country. There was a desert where people lived in walled cities surrounded by sand. The group I was traveling with wanted to cross the desert at night to reach a famous oasis, but the desert was controlled by terrorists or drug cartels that might shoot us on sight. I argued this was a bad idea, we shouldn't go, but everyone else thought we could make it without being seen. Our leader, a handsome older man who looked like George Clooney, kept assuring me we would be fine. I suddenly realized he might be a terrorist or from a cartel himself. So might any of my other traveling companions. It wasn't just the invisible enemy in the desert that I had to fear. I couldn't trust anyone. I didn't want either to go with them or be left behind. Frightened, wondering what to do, not knowing who might harm me, I woke, knowing it is not so very different for us now, in coronavirus times.

A History of Lament

For mothers who've lost children to violence

You would never think so, but the detail is movement.
Not his body, blue beneath the skin, a severed rope
around his waist, the other one fled beyond the high
pure cry of geese over Mt. Ararat with its dirty shawl of snow.
Yes, I have a litany. I can't breathe. I have to go on. Sorrow
does not end. Once, I was the first of my kind, the first lover
of flowering plants, the water lily, lotus, magnolia.
Not anymore. My solution is the mountain itself, hard
on the outside, hot liquid held at the center. Now I am granite,
flint, myself the mortar and fiery pestle, rocky plates
scraping themselves away. I wear adamant like a cloak.
The one sun that remains sheds his light over crags
and blocks of stone. And a seed splits open in the cleft.
What will become a tree – slowly grows.

Physics After He Leaves

If hydrogen and oxygen
if liquid, if silver
if the water of my life
runs through my fingers
if night is an ocean
if Shiva spread
his matted hair
to catch the Ganges
as she fell, if the fall
is broken, if my hands
form a hull
If hot young stars
consume stellar
clouds, if slippage
if enormous, if enigma
if a siren and her song
If darkness
If the Calabash Nebula
packs itself with seeds
if they sow themselves
in dust, in swirls
in star-fields
If space is a garden
and time is a plough
if the line turns
wanders to the river
water's falling still
if not here
then elsewhere
in snake curves
of space-time

If only this moment
if only now exists
this is not the end
this is unending

Wish

Ella was a good-natured child who asked for very little
so when she begged me to take her to a wishing well
I waited until the rain had passed, then drove to a shopping mall.

It was a fancy one – there was a Saks Fifth Avenue and a
        Barnes & Noble
and next to Sephora stood an ornate fountain, an elephant
on a circus ball, its trunk spouting water into the air with joy.

Holding onto her stuffed rabbit in one hand, Ella stood beside me
and I placed a penny in her other hand – small and warm.
She drew a breath, squeezed her eyes shut, and threw the coin in.

Narrow rays of sunshine pierced the clouds above us.
The elephant perched motionless, a fine mist spraying around it.
Ella broke the silence, her lip quivering, "It didn't work, Mama."

I took her hand. "I'm sorry, bug," I said, and we walked back to
the car
our boots splashing through the puddles on the sidewalk.
I prayed for a rainbow to appear – a sign of wonder.

I didn't want to think about Santa Claus or the tooth fairy
or how Ella might never have a sister or a brother – I couldn't bear
empty promises, magic disappearing from her world.

"Some wishes take time," I said, "We mustn't lose hope,"
and as the words left my mouth, I knew that I would never stop
believing in miracles and she – my daughter – was living proof.

In January, May

– in January

January light.
My cats sleeping in the sun.
And they say death's real?

>Is it true? Light plays
>on this window web even
>when I'm not watching?

Wounded butterfly,
who else hears your broken wings
flutter on asphalt?

>Stay very quiet.
>Something new has come to hear
>all that "it" cannot.

– in May

Voluptuous May!
Oh world of petty doing
trampling you under!

>Seeing as spiral.
>Sudden, deeper and deeper.
>The lush spring silence.

Is poetry dead?
No words for how cold May rain
surprises the weeds.

>Are words leaving you?
>And yet, this aging garden –
>nothing more profuse.

What is this heartbeat
struggling to be heard above
a raging river?

White Heron

You fly low and certain across the green
valley, white body swimming the humid air.

Is there a lake hidden in this sunset
land where I have lived so long

that I am blind to its mysteries?

Keep watching, your wild wings urge.
As I journey beyond your seeing

ripples from my winged wake leave
flashes of light through the falling dark.

In The Mood

I'm in the mood to create a shaky podium
for a man with shaky, collapsible ideas
who'd keep talking as his world splintered
around him. Once again he'd be so in love
with what he was saying, he wouldn't see
or feel the screws and bolts I had loosened
until he fell, and had become one
with the debris that moments before
had only been scattered utterances
he trusted his trusted followers to follow.
                              My mood
is devoid of forgiveness, so I'm a happy
architect of this disaster, and not amazed
that he's still talking while on the ground,
unable to shut down his insatiable pettiness
or his sprawl of conspiracies and lies.
And where am I? I've already created
a balcony above it all, ready to become
posterity's assistant, sturdy
as my camera's tripod, the bastard
caught forever, his yellow hair on fire.

Sorrow

I ride a horse named Sorrow.
I ride him under sun, under moon.
I ride him over rough hills and the low barrens.
I ride him toward the snow-topped mountains
through the blue rain.
His forefoot is sure as it strikes the ground.
His sides are wet with lather.
His ears are tender as calla lilies
and twist back toward me
when I finally learn to say his name.

Sorrow carries me and I cannot stop him.
He teaches me to ride,
to clutch him with my strong thighs,
to lay my arm against his neck,
to never pull the bit against his soft mouth.
And when it is done
and there is no sun, no moon,
and the blue rain stops,
I leave him in that sacred place where he can rest
in the sweet grass.

Blood

All of us line up at the auditorium door,
Red Cross cards in hand,
to give blood in a time of disaster,
the only thing we can do.
As the washed thermometer slides into my mouth
I look up at the high windows, where plaster angels
painted in gold with shining flutes line the sills.
I can't help wondering where they stood
before the Red Cross moved in. Now it's
gurneys and plastic tubing, nurses with masks
and tired eyes. As I lie down on a gurney
I hold the gaze of an angel,
somehow unterrified
to be up on the edge like that,
stubby wings no guarantee if he falls.

His golden shoulders are ablaze
in the afternoon sun, and it doesn't matter
that the gold glaze covers
a plaster-dust heart.
The sun is beautiful, and the nurses tell me
what I'm doing is so important, thank you thank you.
I relax and squeeze a little foam ball,
and around me a dozen others do the same.
Somewhere, for someone, this will do some good.
Above us the angels look down,
without judgment or promise,
playing their silent flutes.

What I Told Myself

Stop crying for the dead.
Take a shower and wash your hair.
Stop crying for the sick.
Wear a shirt the color of lilacs.
Paint your face the color of a rose –
soft, pink, glowing.
Stop crying for your lost country –
practice smiling in the mirror.
Memorize your poems
so you can always look at the camera.
Drink a glass of wine to calm yourself –
realize it's impossible to stop the tears.
Apologize later.
Tell them you clicked on
"Join meeting," but you couldn't connect –
For a little while, stop crying.
Go count the falling stars,
instead of the deaths.

Get the Picture

Pandemic 2020

A couple thousand puzzle pieces spill onto the table. You need patience, good light, clear vision, and you must concentrate. Tens of thousands die, one by one, while you shelter safe at home. There's no baseball on the radio. Shut the door, sit down and begin. Feel through the odd shapes, one by one, to find edges that fit together to form a frame. Study the picture on the box; it is your roadmap – can you find the road? There is no road. Children are hungry. Everyone is afraid. Tens of thousands are dying, one by one.

Pandemic Spring Morning

I don't see the usual pair of flickers outside the kitchen window
        the morning
the egret sweeps down on magnificent white wings, settles her
        shining feathers

into a slender profile of danger, picks her spindly black-legged way
among rosebushes and snaps up several unsuspecting lizards
        for lunch.

So far, in this valley of the shadow of death, I am on the
        inside looking out.
I have everything I need, want for nothing – and yet, I am afraid.

A musician gone here, a poet there, an actor, a scientist,
        a police officer,
a mother dies alone, a father, brother, sister, daughter, son – gone.

For a time, the tall white bird stands on one leg as if to pose
        for the media.
Then – as suddenly as she appeared – she, too, is gone.

Reasons to Welcome Autumn 2020 to California
in Spite of Politics and the Pandemic

Because a fiery summer, full of chaos and fury, has come to an end.

Because it's not yet winter.

Because of deep purple, dark red, every shade of orange
    and tawny gold.

Because the leaves transform from glory to glory, and the trees
    let them go.

Because, like the trees, you have much to let go.

Because you can count on the neighbor to complain again
    that autumn blows all the leaves from the liquid amber trees
    up and down our street into her yard.

Because of blackberries, pears, pomegranates, pumpkins and
    steamy mugs of tea.

Because it's Halloween, and the mask and the macabre are
    welcomed by all.

Because it's a somber season populated by super heroes,
    skeletons and ghosts.

Because the time has come to light candles against the
    gathering dark.

Stitching Together

I used to craft quilts with goats.
Mom sewed cotton shirts and shifts,
and my turquoise linen wedding dress.
She always begged me
to help her thread the needle
on the ancient, faithful Singer.

Last time I followed a sewing pattern
was forty-nine years ago.
I have a new machine now, all digital.
My daughter invents dancing skirts for friends.
I cut rectangles for masks
from fabric with pink elephants and orange lions.

Even with two pairs of reading glasses,
one on top of the other,
lights turned up, I can barely see
the needle's eye.
I call my daughter.

We sew masks with stars and strawberries,
black squares for her friend, blue fish for her Dad.
I am vindicated for hoarding
old sheets, t-shirts, ribbons and bandanas.
We clothe their faces and manage their fates.

Any Day Now

That cough –
Covid-19 beginning?
Am I hot? Tired?
Tired of cleaning.
I forget for hours at a time
that I am waiting
to get sick.
Inevitable, eventual,
or so they say.

In the meantime,
my personal curves
are definitely not flattening.
My hair has lengthened
along with the days.

I have rechecked my will.
Told my husband and daughter
I love them.
Better to be prepared
than caught in denial.

Then the sun warms me
as I curl on the blue rug
in the dusty beams of the moment
and nap a cat's dream.

I was the person at the wedding

based on a true news story

who infected one hundred and seventy-seven people.
Three dead, so far.
Yes, we should have all worn masks,
but that didn't happen.
Each person decided for themselves.
It's not all my fault.

The event at the Big Moose Inn was lovely, intimate,
only sixty-five guests. I knew she wanted to keep it small.
Dancing was energetic, shrimp and lobster scrumptious.
They had a Princess Cake, my favorite. The green marzipan icing
was a solid footing for the miniature bride and groom.
The Atlantic Ocean glittered sun blue.
My ex-best friend from high school was glowing
as she slow-danced the first waltz with her new husband.

I guess I am responsible for
poisoning their memories.
Her wedding will be a story
that everybody tells.

My funny uncle that I hadn't seen in years
until the wedding?
I will not visit him in Texas, after all.
He joins me every evening as one of three ghosts
who sit on my bed.
A boyfriend from high school
I broke up with in our senior year –
we are together now forever, ironic no?
The Millinocket librarian is the third wraith
in this inverted Ides of March triumvirate.
She wasn't even at the wedding. Not my fault?

Guess I'm Caesar in this, but I lived, they didn't.
Perhaps I'll choose to join them soon,
but not by COVID, apparently.
I was asymptomatic,
except for those sniffles I thought were allergies.
Pestilence, that Horseman of the Apocalypse,
just galloped on by me, laughing,
the Grim Reaper in tow.

Peonies in the Time of Pandemic

I HAVEN'T

been able to write a word about the coronavirus.
It must have been in the wings for years,
waiting to be coronated, such a spikey crown,
ushered in by a horseshoe bat,
or a pangolin (pang go'lin) n.
any mammal of the order Pholidota,
with its broad, overlapping, horny scales,
waiting caged in a wet market to escape and coronate.
I haven't been able to write a word. Instead
I've been writing a children's book on the vowels,
Long a, as in ape. Long a as in day, three days,
soft e as in ten, ten more, sitting zen not voluntarily,
but obediently sheltered-in, watching the leaf blower man
scatter and send leaves to their piles,
spread them to the gutters. Soft e as in spread. I walk
the empty street, double e e,
running like a nerve
straight down the center of town.
A quiet so large it takes up residency
in vacant cafes and local motels. Vacant.
Two a's, one long, one soft.
I'll walk the apocalypse,
The A that says Uh! Apocalypse
and a soft e as in everyone everywhere.

QUARANTINING

I don't want to go outside.
There are sirens out there and red porches,
women in black coats walking masked toward cactuses.
It's too cold. The citrus know this.
I'll stay inside on the wicker loveseat,

sit behind dark sunglasses, incognito, doing nothing,
stare right into the window of someone else's life –
Any sign of movement over there?
The house next door is a gulag of the domestic.
Maybe just plants live there. I count
the orchids, many orchids, probably dying to get out.
There is a talisman hanging against the window.
That's a good sign, and vines climbing the bookcase,
stacks of books falling over like entire cities under siege,
piles of magazines, crannies full of unidentifiable objects,
hat boxes, hot boxes, picnic coolers, and way too many tables.
Maybe a family of tables lives in the house next door –
a deranged artist, a deposed dictator with no filing cabinets,
just cages of chinchillas. Oh, here comes the bulldozer
over the top of the hill, pushing through the invisible virus.
Oh, here comes the mailman in blue mailman pants, up
the steps with something slick. Do not open. Do not touch.
W.H. Auden warned us about this.
He said as I recall: "The aim of writing poetry is to enable readers
a little better to enjoy life, a little better to endure it."

BE TRUE TO THE GARDEN

Sunflowers and old dogs,
astronomers trying to run off
with the star-white jasmine.
There might not be another chance at a world.
Let the children run through the sprinklers.
Above them a virus floats,
trying to land its microscopic space station.

Garden Sutra

Each morning I bathe Buddha
and I swear
he smiles,

sitting there in the garden
still as only sculpted stone can be,
chin down, fingers curved,
meeting in a mudra
like links in a chain,
eyes closed to daylight,
sharp wind, bitter rain,
dew clinging to his eyelashes
through the passing chill of night
after night.

Even so
when I go to fill the basin
of the waterfall beside him
each morning I bathe Buddha
and I swear, he smiles.

It seems petals fall
one by one from every dream.
No matter how I tend it
they fall.

It's a jungle in this garden,
everything's got teeth.
Even stars eat each other
when two galaxies draw near.

I've lost my heart, my hope,
the figs and the roses fail,
the dogs get skunked,
the Big Dipper tilts empty,
the moon turns her face away

But each morning
I bathe Buddha
and I swear, he smiles.

The River Crossing

Did he pay Charon?
Did he have enough money?
Did we take his wallet to the Crematory?

As they entered the Stygian Marsh,
did he find other lost souls
with no coin for the boatman?

My tears are hard and dark
as Nyx, Goddess of the Night,
obscures the passage back
so he might never return.

Was there enough starlight
from the Eridanids to lead
him forward on his journey?

We walked the Kortum Trail
last summer through thickets
of bright Persian Blue lupines
and swirling carpets of California poppies.

I think he smiled at the end,
stepping from Charon's skiff
into Elysian Fields of golden flowers.

Today

One day we will learn to live
with our solitude.
It will be borne of health,
not disease.
Your friends will call you
to find out what
made you happy today
and you can say:

I was taking a walk
through the neighborhood
and stopped when I noticed
a hummingbird hovering
over a Bird-of-Paradise,
and for a moment
the earth fluttered.

The Invisible

After "Cape Cod Morning" by Edward Hopper (1950)

It doesn't really matter what she's looking at,
be it a rabbit or a fox running across the field.
The truth is, the creature has now become a thought:
her husband, gone for over an hour
when he said he would only be running into town
to pick up a newspaper and a jar of honey.
She was having a hard time sleeping
and the only antidote to her insomnia
(or so she thought) was a cup of warm milk,
and merely watching the honey drip into it,
the thick gold strand being absorbed
by the warm, white liquid, was enough
to calm her, to even allow her to enjoy
being alone in the kitchen at 2 AM.

She barely hears the green Buick as her husband
drives it up the path, the sound of the gravel
as familiar to her as the ticking of the kitchen clock.
He tells her he was delayed because he ran into Bill –
his son just shot in Korea, and he and his wife
awaiting word about his condition. She snaps to,
mumbles something about the state of the world,
all the talk about a nuclear bomb and she wonders
if they'll ever be safe, even here in Cape Cod
where tonight she can only imagine the waves
crashing over each other again and again,
the moon disappearing into each fold.

The Genie

The dancing girl in the yellow silk pants
shimmered in my dream.
She was a flame that kept burning in the morning.
If I bring her to Aladdin,
I can gaze into her chocolate eyes
and lose myself in the maze of her footsteps.

Aladdin thinks I am his servant
but every morning I weave a dream
into the world where he walks by the river.

I hold my prism in the river of sunlight,
each wave of color a possibility
to weave footsteps into the world
I paint every morning.
I can dream or disappear
into the longing for the light
that becomes invisible
inside the bronze of my lamp.

Every morning, you choose
to dance or disappear.

Prayer to the Invisible

I write your name where no one can read it.
In the sky behind a cloud
on a stone
in the footprints of a tortoise walking back
into the ocean.
In the conversation where you came in a dream
from the other place.
When I told you how much I missed you,
you let me know that you can do even more healing
where you are now, out of your body.

A year after the synagogue shooting,
you embrace your friends at the Tree of Life
as they are saying Kaddish for you –
where we sit all day and name the dead.
You whisper to your wife
who is living in a shadow,
sitting alone on the tapestry sofa
where she sat with you.
Our prayers grow out of the shadow
of necessity. Our music
floats above the burden we carry
even though you want us to release it.

I carry your spirit on my shoulders
as I walk into the synagogue
where we played music for you,
as I follow an eclipse north
as I walk into a dream.
I write your name in the sky after midnight
in the Leonid meteor showers,
in the penumbra of an eclipse
of the wolf moon.

Your name is inside the music
I play for you on my cello.
I write your name in the invisible
where you disappeared that morning
where your spirit flew into a cloud.
I write your name
in an ice halo around the moon
and my prayer that this planet
will one day, like an amaryllis,
bloom again.

Turtle Island

What if the world
    was created by a giant turtle
        swimming across the sky
            at the beginning of time?

What if the turtle
    carried dreams in her belly,
        giving birth to fish and stars?

What if the high flying tern
    marked the world lines of space and time
        with nets of aurora borealis?

What if the donkey said
    the humans are a joke, spinning through space
        juggling fire and ice?

What if the crab said
    crawl sideways if you want to uncover
        the dreams that are painted inside of shells?

What if the moon said
    the night will tell you secrets
        if you listen to the music inside of stones?

What if the shark said
    you will discover fish that glow like lanterns
        in deeper currents of ocean water.

What if the octopus said
    your dreams are tentacles
        into a future filled with fish and golden apples.

What if the turtle
    keeps swimming out of the sky
        to a universe hidden somewhere else?

What if the buffalos
    stampede with their ancestors across the Great Plains
        under an ocean of sky?

Buffalo Woman says
    the world is a dream or nightmare.
        Weave your visions with tender hands.

River of Nights and Days

I slept late
into a bad dream.
I'm sure you were in it,
as was my dog in the guise
of another dog.
I'm not sure whether you were
yourself or my sister,
upbeat and annoying,
calm or angry,
but you were my constant companion.

Whatever the trouble was,
we couldn't agree on anything,
except that it was bad
and we didn't know what to do.
I wanted to say to you,
let's live to dream,
but I knew it would upset you,
the realist.
As if we could
you would have muttered.

Awake, I see on our faces
the many currents
of the river of nights and days,
my mirror sister,
and I know unease
will be the constant low voice
of many months to come.

New Year's Day, 2021

Some days I am productive, a habit I cultivated against the dreariness of the pandemic. Doing things makes time pass. Most days I wash clay off my hands from the pinch pot I just made and go straight to macrame, knotting repetitions to make imperfect webs.

I sweep floors, do the laundry, pay bills. But today, I think about doing things but never get around to it. The day is bright and clear and cold. I can hardly wait for it to be over, for night to come, a time of relieved self-forgiveness with the tv on, and then to bed with a crossword puzzle or a murder mystery, taking passivity to its end goal, sleep. I think *when will this year end* when I catch myself, *it has*. Is this a new beginning? It doesn't feel different so far; 2020 will continue for a while.

> we talk repeating
> what's not new
> a squirrel's life
> going back and forth
> along a telephone line

Tangled Threads

All the tangled threads of the day. What am I doing? What am I
going to do? I lose track of what I think I should be doing, but
I am grateful to practice macrame. The intricate patterns absorb
me. I make mistakes, retrace my steps, rip it out and redo. I like
unknotting almost as much as knotting. It feels good to fix things,
a meditation for these times.

> untying knots
> trying for perfection
> these slow days
> I weave webs
> to be swept away

Easter with Pandemic

It's easy to mistake faith for sunshine,
hope with the new grass and pink tulips.

We celebrate alone, outside the stone boxes
we call "church." We may pray or dye eggs.

Resurrection: what we cling to when our bodies
fail us, when we watch crowds taken away

to be buried. The stone will not be rolled away
for them. How can we sing in such a blighted land?

On the pale green willows we hung up our harps.
Sugar on the tongue, praise in our songs

but in our hearts we wonder: how long will you
forsake us, O Lord? And the ambulance wails in the night.

We wait for a cure, a vaccine, a sign. We wait for someone
we can call *Rabboni,* my teacher. We wait for someone
        to quiet us with

their love, to rejoice over us with singing. The sun rises
over a hilltop. We wait, impatient, for a return.

Cry the Beloved Monarch

The Aztecs believed the dead return
as clouds of butterflies,
floating spirits of wispy plumes
to visit the living
each year for a single day.

When 10,000 butterflies dropped
like speckled rain in an acrid East Coast fog,
people mourned as they collected
scores of delicate corpses littering the ground.
They did not demand penalties
for the killing mists used for mosquitoes
or the collateral death of visiting spirits.

World attention also turned elsewhere
when Monarch forest keepers in Michoacan
were murdered for protecting
the sacred nesting shrines from illegal loggers.

The Aztecs believe each person dies three separate deaths.
The first when the body exhales its last breath,
the second when loved ones bury us to rejoin earth mother,
and the third, when no one is left alive to whisper our name.

We inch ourselves toward that final death
along with orange and blue Monarchs,
plot our own extinction,
forever forgotten.

Tangelos I Devoured With Wine and Chocolate in Quarantine

When the virus came I had to learn touch via the internet,
as the world stopped and bowed
before an invisible enemy.

I became afraid of the mailman and his fingers
on hundreds of pieces of junk mail
before setting some in my box.

I became afraid *for* the mailman.

Treating the sick and vulnerable,
health workers became health soldiers
until they too carried the unseen.

I want to tell you that I love you
and for the first time, I spent Easter alone
and made bean and cheese tostadas.

When we hug again,
I want to share the blessings of the morning light
and the cardinal pair that comes each morning to my bird bath.

I want to tell you
that my cousin's painting is called, "Urge to Go"
and that real silence
is speech that can't be articulated.

When I come back to noise, I will be a pilgrim
that made a new story
with courage in its center,
a reverberating bell.

I want to share that the new horizon
will be in the form of a stranger
with a cargo full of revelation,
scared to death at the edges.

I want to tell you to be a sunflower
searching as the sun beckons its gaze.

Essential

His name, one of those monosyllabic manly names –
Bob or Curt or Frank – I asked once when I caught
up to his mail truck. His smile, a bulging manila
envelope of good cheer, determination, irony,
maybe a secret. He used to stop along the route
to shmooze with a guy or two but these days
he just keeps going.

I'm disguised crown to chin by a floppy hat,
sunglasses, mask but recognized by the psychedelic
cane I carry like Dumbo's feather. He no longer
sees my smile but hears me scream Thank You!
as he careens around the corner, and we salute
one another with thumbs up, each thumb
an Olympic torch of praise and celebration.

For Nina Rose

Once upon a time when the plague descended,
when numbers numbed our brains
and images made us cry out to our screens
in grief and horror, when we longed for
and feared full breaths, crunchy salads,
loving hugs, when storm clouds and blue
shared a sky, when trees were bathed
in golden light and shrouded in shadow,
you puddle splashed in an oversized
raincoat and pink rubber boots,
content to snuggle in the animal warmth
of Mama and Big Sister, made serious
sounds as you turned pages in an
upside-down book, a one-and-a-half-
year-old tottery penguin falling and
pushing yourself up with a triumphant smile.
They said you wouldn't remember
the dark but I saw you shake the iron
gate, desperate for escape, your nearly
brand-new body already an encyclopedia
of once upon a time.

Conversing with My Mirror

A prevalence of quiet
inspires contemplation.

My morning mirror asks,
"How are you today?"

I answer, "I am on the edge
of dying or living –
My choice."

I've watched hatred grow,
inciting mobs to insurrection.

I am on the verge
of hating or loving –
My choice.

Hate destroys; Love creates.
Hate dies; Love lives –
My choice.

Then my mirror asks,
"What choice are you making
now?"

The Woodsmen

Working puzzles at the table
between the honing of the saw-blades –
the cutting of the forest

we fit the pieces together.
Birds flew from the woods –
deer fled –

we followed –
believing stories
when we had hooves and horns and wings.

Dissected

In a puzzle game
you took a piece of rock-face from the mountain
and placed it in the sky.
You brought the clouds to earth those rainy afternoons
my brother and I walked in galoshes
in the slough
before the drought of dry season in high summer.
Through a slice of windshield
you drew the open plains.
The sail of a cloud.
The distant sea.

Switching Places

I pore over puzzle pieces, longing
to connect the flat paperboard cutouts
into tongue and groove combinations calling forth
a jigsaw riverboat paddling the Missouri,
or a southwestern pepper fair, people dancing.

For hours I can be in someone else's picture.

Mine is a raging pandemic, fierce wildfires,
and months of shelter-in-place, while outside,
a thirsty lawn suffers from drought and my neighbor's
thread bare COVID-19 mask clings to rocks between driveways,
six-feet-away from everything.

Homebound

It's impossible to be anywhere else.
The galaxy always travels with me.
We are strung together, like the spine
of a suitcase hurling through space,
a star running away from its stellar nursery.

Tucked into the luggage lining of this solar system,
I am held – a full moon humming – by gravity.
But when the unsettling force of a black hole
jostles me back and forth, I pick a spot in the Milky Way,
slide a straw in and drink up.

Prayer for Noah's Passing

Last night, Noah came to me.
He seemed to be on a long journey.
He was carrying water and talking about the water,
but after that it wasn't clear and he disappeared.
It was before midnight and I had a dream.
At the time I didn't realize it was Noah.
He was talking about the water for the journey.
I think it was when Noah was leaving for his journey.
I think that Kannon-sama was with him.
I have Noah's muffler on the altar to Kannon-sama
wrapped in a ribbon, with a card.
I know that he went to heaven, so don't worry.
My love goes to you.

The Last Supper

At the last supper I had Vanilla Shake
while my brother had Fillet-O-Fish
and Large Fries, and between my slurps
and his salty swallows, we told every
childhood story we could remember.

For the next day he was going into a home,
which, though he said it would be the end
of him, he had come to agree he could no
longer take care of himself. And, in this time
of contagion and masks, I would not be able
to visit.

So I called it "The Last Supper" –
two white haired men
trying to hold onto
what little time we had left.

Stardust

Some seven years after the cows came
and the dairy began
with its waltz of tails, moo-song and milk,

a car pulled in from the road and an elderly couple
made their way through the gate and into pasture
where the cows lay atop the hill.

All the cows now but one, for as the couple spoke
of how the herd had been theirs, until he, too old
to lift the milking can, retired,

a cow named Stardust stood and with long strides
walked toward us and as he turned to see, she
placed her head in his arms,

and his wife said, "Stardust was his favorite."

Today I Wake Up

For Rayne

Today I wake up,
and nothing has a name.
That's what happens
sheltering at home.
All the particulars dissolve.
Edges and hard places
no longer hold up –
powder stirred in water.

Light and wind articulate
a kind of stillness even
as they move. Weighted
in being, moments grow,
and wonder becomes
a given – given gladly.

Then delight, at once tiny
and hefty, whirls about
to touch the reach of living,
that unfolding brightness
dappled nearby. I hear
a humming, thrumming
music of wings.

A Summer Before

I wasn't brave enough when I was four
to walk the long dirt drive under braided elms
to play with the boy next door
that summer we lived in Xenia, Ohio.

But I memorized the dance those black leaves made
on that long dirt drive
and the backlit eyes of the amber-headed boy
standing on his porch with something
bright blue in his hand.

Even at four I knew
that scene would pass
like stone into memory.

And now you, grandson, four years old
stuck inside all day
and very amber yourself
find me in my favorite chair
put a blue toy in my hand
and walk away.

Other memories of that summer...
Fireflies and heat-lightning.
Voices through a window screen.
Rhubarb pie.

Paradise Paused

March 31, 2020 – the day I was supposed to fly home

In this sci-fi time of fastened doors and canceled flights
my thoughts return to you, jagged edge of ocean.

Sitting up in bed with one little light
I find myself standing high on your cliff,

ice plants clinging to fog and sandstone,
marking the boundary between now and never.

I watch you smash against everything solid,
wearing away every shiny surface. Or is it

a polishing of stillness? Isn't that
what they're asking of us?

If only fear wasn't eating peace, if only time itself
wasn't a valid question, maybe then

I'd feel serene imagining you and your blue under blue,
gulls sailing overhead, a line of whales spouting salty plumes,

someone shouting "Two O'clock!," turning all our heads to see,
feel that burst in the chest that means we are alive,

here, on the edge looking out as far as we can see.
If only those wildflowers, those damned red wildflowers,

weren't approaching from behind, their blossomed shadows
cast over our sleepless dreams, our once beautiful forever.

Easter Eve, 2020

Walking in our distanced neighborhood
our dog on her leash, us on ours,
we run across a family of three.

The child in her bunny suit,
the mother in bunny-like sweats,
the father, may all the gods bless him,

dressed in what is the most
Easter bunny costume he could find:
a head-to-toe to-ears-to-pouch

kangaroo. We laugh, take their picture
from at least 6 feet away and go our way.
They are the first and last people we see all day.

I hope they return tomorrow,
a congregation of three
asserting *We're alive!, come what may.*

March 31

On April Fools' eve
I'd like to wake tomorrow
and find it's a joke.

Day 5 Shelter in Place

Late afternoon in my own backyard
another community of weeds
I shall conquer. Beneath a pink
lemon tree alive in the gossip
of pollen and buzz. These buttery
leather gloves protect from
thorns or spiked intruders.

They make me think of dad
walking around the circus lot
during setup or teardown,
as sweat dribbled across his brow,
I too feel the heat of summer's
promise upon my back. All birds

oblivious to this pandemic, just
going about their spring rituals
instinctively creating a new
generation. All feels quite safe
and innocent in this moment.

Leaf shadows and fragrant riots
paint me into their corner.
Mother's Cecile Brunner is in
her full glory, a snowy chandelier

draping the crepe myrtle. What
comes next? More uncertainty
on the global effect yet somehow
this little patch of nature gifts
me a temporary calm.

Circus

an abecedarian experience

Acrobats have many angels
balanced precariously on
clouds of silver above
death defying feats where
every audience member's
face is frozen in
ghostlike wonderment,
high-wire wizardry
illuminates the skyline
jugglers, fire eaters, clowns
kidding around keep eyes confused
like two stray
marbles rolling in opposite
navigation, so much to
observe it can be difficult to
pinpoint every somersault or
quickened gesture of practiced
refinement, the entire hippodrome a
spectacle of spinning fiery magic
time and time again townsfolk gather
under the stars to gasp and pray
vehemently for the safety of each
woman, man, and child they behold like
X's and O's tossed in impossible directions
you truly have to see it to believe it
zany and miraculous, the circus in our soul.

Pandemic Cocoon

if you wanted to visit us
as we waited for death in one of the rooms
along the hospital corridor
you would be told that it would be okay
as long as you wore a mask
wore it always no matter what
as long as you covered
your nose and chin
and let nothing in no matter what

I'm exhausted with being careful
in the afternoon they would move us
out into the hall in our wheelchairs
and leave us there for hours
couldn't hold hands with neighbors right or left
couldn't hold life in our bodies
had to reject anybody not wearing a mask
felt like a chrysalis drying up, in a cocoon

when you're in the chair,
and you've been parked there a long time
you can escape by dying
but some of us don't
some move back into our rooms
to be with great spirit
enjoying the butterflies
flying peacefully
into the shining light

Today, When I Could Do Nothing

March 17, 2020

Today, when I could do nothing,
I saved an ant.

It must have come in with the morning paper,
still being delivered
to those who shelter in place.

A morning paper is still an essential service.

I am not an essential service.

I have coffee and books,
time,
a garden,
silence enough to fill cisterns.

It must have first walked
the morning paper, as if loosened ink
taking the shape of an ant.

Then across the laptop computer – warm –
then onto the back of a cushion.

Small black ant, alone,
crossing a navy cushion,
moving steadily because that is what it could do.

Set outside in the sun,
it could not have found again its nest.
What then did I save?

It did not look as if it was frightened,
even while walking my hand,
which moved it through swiftness and air.

Ant, alone, without companions,
whose ant-heart I could not fathom –
how is your life, I wanted to ask.

I lifted it, took it outside.

This first day when I could do nothing,
contribute nothing
beyond staying distant from my own kind,
I did this.

Because this is California,

after I pour my morning cup of coffee,
I refresh the fire incident map
then check the air quality app.

The sky is tea-colored and
I'm not sure if I should go for a stroll,
work in the garden
or stay shut indoors.

Because this is California,
Burning Man celebrants crowd Ocean Beach despite
the ban on large gatherings during the pandemic,
and a conflagration is ignited by pyrotechnics
at a gender-reveal party (It's a boy!)

We're all edgy in the sixth month
of this rift in our routines,
but because this is California,
we think we deserve a break –
more than, say, Nebraska or Alabama.

Because this is California,
we know there's a giant snoring beneath the ground
who might waken any day.

Because this is our home, our Golden State,
we roll over in bed and check the latest Nixle alert,
then go back to sleep to the lullaby of tanker planes.

March 17 Lockdown

An eerie silence in the land,
all traffic maps green?
How long
has it been since
we've seen such freedom!

And yet it's not.

This Fitful Life

After my father died my mother told me, "Life is not fair."
All around life was not fair in that time of the Vietnam War,
wounded or maimed boys, firefights, dead children,
farmers in a hamlet, emerging from the darkness
of assassinations, riots, protests, social injustice,
revolutions, and personal teenage angst, the betrayal
of love. Somehow, we go on despite deaths,
terrorism, pandemics, a world gone mad.
How is it that this unfair life still offers hummingbirds,
honey-drizzled mornings, iced coffee on a porch swing,
almond croissant in hand? First sunbeams light
the basil, dill, and parsley pots staggered on front steps,
geraniums in flower boxes, a blue heron stretched across sky.
Mom, I know life is not fair but far better to know
is the light of hope, the days before us quietly unreeling,
nights still holding the impossible moon.

Free Fall

As the world reels,
your future is dissolving
like salt in a broth.
You sit at home, watch the snow
sifting through the branches,
the light and crows.

In the quiet of empty hours
you think about those that have flown.
Your offerings to them
are those you want for yourself:
a fine red wine, cheese of sheep's milk,
marmalade of limes.

The earth and silence welcome you;
nothing between you
and the stars' cool fire.
Worlds float up from your words.

Fear loosens its hold, but bruises remain.
You lie with your hand resting
on the place of acceptance
along the curve of your ribs.

The pen, paper, the bowl of fruit
are your companions.
Words are written, deleted,
unfinished...

In a Time of Corona

With a line from Joanna Klink.

I left camellias for you
        by the stone bridge –

                pink into white petals

circling the multitudes
        of ovules yellow as late corn.

                I did not pluck them

like a feather thief
        from their leathery beds

                but gathered blooms

from where they'd fallen
        and scattered their bodies

                across the capstones.

Don't be afraid
        to touch them. The day

                will always be full

of reasons to stop
        breathing. Lie down. Lie down

                and feel the *rivers shift,*

blue veins through soil.
        Place a petal on each eye.

        Let them blush you

into waking. Let them say you met my passing
        with a kiss, their skins,

        soft and veined as yours.

Camino de Santiago – Journey of the Dead, Day 23, April 2020

A woman changes her newborn in the open air

>   next to the felled oak
>   where the moss grows thick as thunder

Wind shakes the copse as the infant looks up

>   into the undulating branches
>   feels a mother's breath on its brow

When she smiles the child's heart beats

>   in tandem with hers
>   and in the tree's rings

a song of human hours plays back

>   on the grooves
>   softer than the sound leaves make

when they inhale our breath

>   Life makes a fool of death's edges –
>   that's all we know

Neowise Arrives After 6,000 Years on the Tail of Covid-19

By Lois P. Jones

After the long black road twists
round itself and the mountains
are shadow puppets cut
from their crossbar. After the search
for blackout among the masked,
some with telescopes or binoculars
some in large crowds
their faces naked as copper kettles
around their circle of light.
After I take my walking stick
to the hillside where the valley below
is lit in a festival of fireflies –
  the houses never left
  the families and backyard pools
the cars sparking down
the freeway dark, I try to see
you with my eyes but you are
an imaginary sketch of light –
yet you are there next to the dim
red flash of the tower.
I raise my field glasses and catch
your full-blown sparkle –
a tassel of light above two stars
as your gold mesh tail fans out -
finless like me, swimming hard
in the deep.

Neowise

By Susan Rogers

It bloomed from my fingers
in the dipper dark under Ursa Major
among a constellation of faint lights
scattered in the heavens
like the tips of tiny petals
of a white rose.
I held it as long as I could
blooming in between
my thumb and index finger
so I could feel the pulse
of 6,800 years coursing through me.
I have been waiting
longer than even I know
for a white rose to spill
itself into my galaxy
into this year lost in oblivion
into my new unfathomable wisdom.

Tactile

It has been twelve months
since I have felt your touch.

Your voice is cello-rich
over Zoom, but something
is missing in your eyes.

Doubt feathers my clavicle;
I crave the language of tenderness
pressing my shoulder.

The ache of emptiness –
a lyric of sweetbriar and wild
roses stings my skin.

How long will it take to lose
the muscle memory of our
spines curled in unison?

I slip in and out of dreams,
untethered without filaments
of your gold-brown hair.

I long for your chai-spiced kiss,
and shiver with this thing
called skin hunger.

I worry the distance
is dousing our flame.

I feel an abyss of grief for us,
for all the lives that never had
a second chance ... yet, we are alive.

Come back, love. I will wait,
and wait, and wait, for us.

Autumn Pastorale

The house looms like a lion
that growls and snaps
clenched air. How small the room
where I breathe. Even smaller
the chair I sit in for hours.

But I'm not angered by this smallness
invading me. I hoard the sun's rays
caught in leaves,
drink the shadows of trees.

I watch thin spiders seeking refuge
in corners and the dust of stars
settling in eaves. Stillness gasps
between sill and lintel.

Poetry and a cup of pale wine
mute the times, masking egos,
as news pummels and stings like hail.
Ancient stones cool the fevered body.

The flutes of autumn blow a pastorale
and the woods speak. They feed
the soul and tangled dreams
while the face of the moon,
white as a ghost,
watches the house shift.

Pandemic Moon, March, 2020

The moon was in self-isolation, too,
and wearing a white mask as it passed us
in an aisle of the night, keeping a distance,

not acknowledging us. It was pushing
a cart heaped up with stars, far more stars
than any moon could ever need, the cart

sparkling, a few little stars falling out,
left behind as the moon rolled past,
on its way toward eternity's checkout.

Gaia's Prayer to Her Children

May you discover again the order of things.
After snowdrops, skunk cabbage.
Bloodroot before furry yellow coltsfoot.
Don't even think about morels
until tender May apples
open their green umbrellas.

Hard rains fill the lowest places first.
Ditches, gullies and dry runs flood
before the creek becomes a roiling river,
the hillside a thundering cataract
the street where you live
a swirling Ahab sea tossed with broken trees.
Next hour, next day when the mailbox is packed with mud,
discover brown trout flopped on the driveway.
Next week, spinach from your washed-out garden
sprouts in your neighbor's lawn.

You cannot know what you do not live.
Take off your boots.
Your gloves.
Your glasses.
Turn out the lights.
Let the animals who taught you
how to feed yourselves
walk through your dreams.

Pandemic, Day Two

Nine AM daily run past the Sausalito
Ferry: two cars crouched in a lot where
two hundred slumbered yesterday,
past the closed front doors of the Fudge
Shop, the No Name Bar, 2Bella Boutique,
mannequins in the window flashing me
glassy smiles, past three masked walkers
six feet apart on the long promenade
just above the Bay.

The front door of my life locked too,
shut down for a duration of indeterminate
end. My life: the hugs, the loving hands,
(oh, the loving hands), the classes,
the agendas, the lingering lunches,
the monthly meetings, the movies
the ballet (oh, the ballet), cruising
aisles at Safeway, cruising air currents
out of SFO – all shut down now

and apart from the daily anxiety prods:
USA deaths top 2100
Fauci predicts 200,000
Why doesn't Mike answer his phone?
Can I touch my newspapers?
Can I touch my mail?
Still .... still, nothing I have to do
nowhere I have to be ....
Time, my tireless driver, stretched out,
snoozing in the back seat,

and I, a child again, home sick from
school, the day unfolding before me
long and lazy as a cat – some snacks
to keep me happy, sufficient story books
at my side to ease me right on through
to next year. A new life, yes, provided
I survive, and one I could get used to
very fast.

What's Sent Our Way

"How does one endure, survive, adapt, accept with grace what's sent our way?" – Poet Lynda Hull, in a letter written to her student, S.A.

We must *endure* –
We rise each morning to the same sounds.
Birds among motors. At times just noise,
but now a welcome reminder – we are still here.

We must *survive*:
It was never easy to maneuver through all the tricks and facades
learned through the years – they all worked, up until now.

We must *adapt*:
In our evolving lexicon a new C word, more horrifying than the other.
Corona – it can be beautiful:
A pearly glow surrounding the darkened disk of the moon.
Yet, every beautiful thing decays, even gilded points of
            a crown wear thin.

We must *accept:*
Everywhere an absence, only to see
the cloaks of orange and black monarchs
their black wing-tipped eyes,
staring down at amazed empty spaces,
of buildings and bike racks, and the silence of blazing bus horns.

And then there's *grace:*
This the hardest part – to relinquish power, and with
            sweeping wings,
fall to land into the hurdle, then attempt to rise in the face
of *what's sent our way.*

Poem to My Unborn Grandchild in Covid-19 Times

When I think future,
it's a wisp of thought on the wing
of the lone monarch hovering
and unleashing an imagined tomorrow
around the milkweed.

What will you see of this world?

Today, in the quiet of distance,
the world blooms against the trill
of a yellow-rumped warbler and cicadas at dusk.
The dormant bougainvillea surprises me
with a purple thrush of crested petals.

How will this world crown you?

A child arriving in these times,
learning to embrace the future
in tiny conceived moments.

Darnella's Duty

Darnella Frazier is the young woman who filmed the murder of
George Floyd on May 25, 2020

How does it feel to be 17,
and just want to hold your life in your
glistening palm, go to the corner
and buy a sparkling water to quench
a parched mouth that longs to sing?

How does it feel to witness
a purpose too cruel
for all your 17 rotations
around a sun you only want to bask in?

How does it feel to beg a name,
to witness a life breaking,
while your opened eyes
see loss and corruption corralled
to the borderless sky?

And how does the humid wind feel
as you watch it carry one man's life
to a crevice where only the wind can go?

Portal

Confined to home during the pandemic
and craving company besides each other's,
we turn to the bathroom window
that opens onto our neighbors' driveway.
The portal, we call it.
Every day at two in the afternoon,
we wedge ourselves between toilet and wall
to unlatch the old-fashioned lock
and swing wide the glass in its sturdy frame.
A small opening, but enough.
Whatever the weather, Jim and Laura
are standing there on the pavement,
sometimes leaning against their car,
the designated distance between us.
They talk about their daughter in New York,
holed up and safe, their son across the bay,
working from home and playing old board games.
Our circle of worry differs.
No kids of our own, but my mother
at nearly eighty-nine a prime target,
though Iowa not as hard hit as here.
For once, I'm glad she's far away.
The ordinary is now scarce:
toilet paper, rubbing alcohol, eggs,
flour, sugar. Yeast almost unheard of.
Laura and Matthew swap menus –
food the quarantine's welcome distraction.
Nothing too serious at the portal.
No death toll rising, no shortage
of medical tests or supplies,
no danger in the everyday
we used to take, unthinking, for granted.

Scrub

This morning, a jay
alights on the ragged
rose bush near my window,
bright seed in its beak
and wings like a brilliant scrap
of saved-up October sky.
This hard year almost over.
And now a bird reminds me
how beauty can scour us clean.

Masked

Swathed in cotton scarf, latex gloves,
only inches of skin remain uncovered.
I prepare for walks like an astronaut
about to exit protective capsule,
fragile body ejected into perilous space.

Grocery shopping was once an exercise
in selecting unblemished fruit, organic vegetables,
visiting with cashiers and neighbors.
Now it is the equivalent of the hunger games,
all of us unwilling tributes, trying to survive
the newly lethal environment.

I am the invisible woman,
possibly a bank robber, cattle rustler,
or tempting seductress,
expression inscrutable as I venture forth
beneath my cloaking mask.

Golden Buddha

You are Golden Buddha. You are the light
Of the world. I say this in my head to
Everyone. A fine electrical night

Hums with water, carbon molecules, through-
Out the Eastern Seaboard. Computers fail
In morning, a cool day, a brilliant blue

For miles. I don't see you much in the pale
Light. You are my other soul. In the night,
We lie next to each other for hours: ale

Bottles, groves of trees dripping with light,
A waterfall lit by lanterns: babies
Cry in their own language lit by the tight

Hooks and loops of alphabet, flower dyes
Soaked to color the body, soul, and sky.

Break

We put the puzzle together piece
by piece, loving how one curved
notch fits so sweetly with another.
A yellow smudge becomes
the brush of a broom, and two blue arms
fill in the last of the sky.
We patch together porch swings and autumn
trees, matching gold to gold. We hold
the eyes of deer in our palms, a pair
of brown shoes. We do this as the child
circles her room, impatient
with her blossoming, tired
of the neat house, the made bed,
the good food. We let her brood
as we shuffle through the pieces,
setting each one into place with a satisfied
tap, our backs turned for a few hours
to a world that is crumbling, a sky
that is falling, the pieces
we are required to return to.

Joy

Even when the gods have driven you
from your home, your friends, the tree
you planted brought down by storm,
drought, chain saw, beetles, even

when you've been scrubbed
hollow by confusion, loss,
accept joy, those unbidden
moments of surcease –

the quiet unfolding
around your shoulders
like a shawl, the warmth
that doesn't turn to burning.

When the itch has stopped, the cough,
the throb, the heart's steady beat
resumed, the barn door

open to the shade, the horse inside
waiting for your touch, apple
in your pocket pocked, riddled

the last to fall, the season
done. As you would accept
air into your lungs, without
thinking, not counting

each breath. As you accepted
the earth the first time you stood
up on it and it held you, how it was

just there, a solid miracle,
gravity something you would
learn about only later
and still be amazed.

In Any Event

If we are fractured
we are fractured
like stars
bred to shine
in every direction,
through any dimension,
billions of years
since and hence.

I shall not lament
the human, not yet.
There is something
more to come, our hearts
a gold mine
not yet plumbed,
an uncharted sea.

Nothing is gone forever.
If we came from dust
and will return to dust
then we can find our way
into anything.
What we are capable of
is not yet known,
and I praise us now,
in advance.

A House of Bones

I sit waist-high in a wheelchair.

My head tilts left —
and my body curves,
a slanted *S*.

Motion glides
through my hands —

as language blooms infinite colors —
to light a house of bones.

Wind Songs

Wind is a separate story
each crisp Ponderosa Pine, elder musing cedars,
capricious willow flocks, starlit stones, shadowed creeks
appear as letters, thoughts,
whispered dreams from tall grass prairies
weave to stanzas of belonging,
to everything she touches,
captures my chilled feet and chafed heels
in Wolf Creek's wondrous waters.

Time . . . and Time Again

Carpe diem, quam minimum credula postero: "Seize the day,
putting as little trust as possible in the future." – Horace

Back home from the airport
after a cancelled flight
Fog whispering the secret
of the next 24 hours in my ears
Time sheds like fairy dust around
the telephone, computer and front door
Even the rabbits and cat
in the backyard expect nothing
until the neighbor comes tomorrow

Carpe diem, quam minimum credula postero
I remove my wristwatch
Cover the kitchen wall clock
Silence the Black Forest cuckoo
The incessant alarm that every
second, minute, hour brings closer
the moment our own tick stops

This day will not be stolen by cold facts
Not when the sun in its circle of life
warms with golden arms through the window
And when a candle breathes the energy
of orange blossom spring into the air

The banana tree in the atrium
that has come full bloom waits to be picked
The ready-to-be-recycled inner core
of the tree chopped into pieces for pulp
The slow dance of a papermaker
accompanied by Mozart
Who was so driven that maybe he never
had a block of metronome-free time

I hope he did have dark chocolate and the sin
of red wine while the sun was still young
The swoon of exhaustion and the sweet taste
of satisfaction that a perfected craft sparks
A hundred deckle-edged sheets and I'm on fire

At midnight I make amends with Time
over dinner of oatmeal and ice cream
Invite it into the bedroom
for a glass of limoncello, chapters of Zane Grey
And when light is swallowed into the belly of night
its heart no longer beats death's war drum
An ally now whose hands break
the 2:00 a.m. ice of aloneness

Whose voice sings a sleep mantra
assuring that my flame hasn't flickered still
That the sun will be born again
Day will look through the window
That Time will wring the water
from the handmade papers in their passage

As Decreed   By the Invisible

Forget the promise of May   in Venice
though your honey's been planning it   for many a moon
Forget the *Palazzo* you've stayed in before
its third floor view   of the Grand Canal
Forget the gondolas   the water taxis   the *vaporetti*
They're not overflowing   with laughing crowds   not gliding through
the waterways   They're all tied up at their piers
Their handlers are sheltering in place
So are you   You won't be
wending your way   through narrow streets
across arched bridges   to an intimate restaurant
by a small canal   where you and your love will watch
light fade   dusk fall   while drinking a shimmering
Veneto blanco   and feasting   on *risotto del mare*
The restaurant is closed   The chef is feverish   coughing
feels like an elephant   has stomped on his chest   There is no bed
for him   in the hospital   The air is heavy laden
with the agony   I see   I   who can't be seen
though I'm running   the show
though I wear a golden crown   a halo   a corona
though I shake the leaves   whip up the air   that belongs
to us all   passes through lungs   into bloodstreams   and trees
into everything that is   including me   I sparkle
in Venetian glass   gather droplets
of sneeze   scatter the virus
you'll never know   whose vital force   will ebb away   next

Truth be told   you don't believe in me   don't believe the unseen
has power over all   your brilliant technologies
The joke is   your airplanes   your stock markets
your fancy red car   that talks to you
are all   hiding out from me

Now I'm the boss   Stay home   It's time *not*
to get on an airplane time *not*
to drive through heavy traffic time *not*
to go to very important meetings   It *is* time
to take a slow walk with your sweetie around the neighborhood
It's a glorious day in early spring time to smell

the magnolia blossoming outside
the child care center time to delight
in the yellow red and purple jungle gym but where
are the children?   Time to contemplate the sign
in the window "How do we end this divisiveness?"

I am not the divider I hold you all in my grip   Look
the sky is a clearer blue than you've seen in many a moon
The Grand Canal is running clear full of fish it is said dolphin leap
in the estuary   I give you time
to sit in your yellow velvet chair to visit with
the dark skinned bride you helped dress
in a dream   She wanted a slinky tight white gown
through which her skin would glow   This gorgeous
visitor from the unseen has come to help you see
joy in terrible times   You wonder
Where is the groom?   She says

You're breathing   the unseen beloved
                        is in your lungs
                                is in your heart
                                    is everywhere

Sheltering in Place with Steely Dan

I discover more of God
in my Hoka running shoes
than in the words of Hosea. Vultures
perched on my neighbor's gutter
look at me with disgust. "All this time,"
they say, "and not a single poem
in *Poetry Magazine*." "Only a fool would say that,"
croons Donald Fagen. I turn up the volume
to breaking news on MSNBC. Another shooting and why
doesn't someone wave an AK-15
at those red-faced buzzards pretending to be eagles
while devouring a half-million people. I curse again
and again, placing an order with Amazon
for a Whole Foods pickup. It really sucks
when I can't find a delivery time
in my zip code. For months I've been running low
on mental health. My therapist says it's endemic
among groups that believe salvation
is predestined. We need disease to grow
the way a kernel of corn needs a dead fish
dropped into the hole where it's planted. I learned that
in grade school studying about American Indians
and their contribution to our great nation. "Thanks
for all the fish" were the last words whistled by dolphins
in *The Hitchhiker's Guide to the Galaxy*.
I want a better way to say goodbye
than "Drink your big black cow and get outta here."
But I have to run. God is waiting.

Tanka

Today
I do not need any food
75th birthday
For the next quarter century
I'll be a lovetarian

Substitutions for Buttermilk

Shelter in Place Day 16, Spring 2020

Find acid to induce curdling– lemon or vinegar
        so many things taste sour nowadays

Let sit for 15 minutes
        how quickly things can change

Is half and half a better approximate?
        I was only allowed one
        jug of milk at the store

Mixing butter and milk won't do it
        just another failure of language,
        like social distancing or camera phone

There wasn't any sugar in the store either
        they say it is like wartime almost,
        victory gardens again, can we do
        without with that much dignity?
        I feel hardly as brave.

Borrowing a cup from the neighbors seems risky
        never have we needed each other more

Maybe I will bake the cake next week
        will we learn anything
        from this practice of waiting?

Maybe it will be safe to go out again before the fires come
        nearby smoke, reason to stay inside,
        reason to prepare to leave quickly

Who has all the buttermilk, the sugar, the money
what are you saving it for?

When was toilet paper even invented?
we existed before it did,
and prison cells, and 2-day delivery, ATMs.

Didn't buttermilk come from what was leftover, anyway?
after this, after all this,
can we make something sweet
from what is left behind?

This is no time for poetry

Poems must keep 2 meters apart
Poems cannot leave their structures
Poems should wear masks
No poems should travel

It is alright for essential poems to travel
Everywhere there's another poem that appears
No gathering of these poems
Only very important poems allowed here

Poems must close their doors
Poems lose their jobs
These poems need money
These other poems need ventilators

The poems keep doubling everyday
We need to flatten the curve of the poems
We need to plank the poems
The poems may have to walk the plank

Distance poems from poems
Find a vaccine for all poems
Wash poems several times a day
Keep these poems away from these poems

Poems are stocking up on poems
These poems must stop price gouging
Interest is falling in poems
Another cruise ship full of poems

Chinese poems
Italian and Spanish poems
French Poems
New York City Poems

Another outbreak of poems
Poems must self-isolate for two weeks
On the radio they keep reading poems
Everyday the prime minister reads poems

Another day, another 10,000 poems
Entitled poems
Untitled poems
No one can revisit these poems

Some poems are put on ice
Poems are buried without any poems
Poems are sent back to work on poems
Apart from other poems

A Second Wave

Here comes another wave of poems
Poems can still fly but cannot drive across the borders of a poem
Time to close the poem to incoming poems
Time to close down the poem

Only essential poems may open for 28 days
Essential Big Box Poems like Walmart, Tim Hortons Coffee
and the Liquor Control Board of Ontario
Poems may be delivered online or picked-up curbside

Poems will be looking a little different this year
Poems must stay apart and only interact
With other poems in their own RV or household
Please stay in your bubble and read only your own poems

Some snowbirds are still planning to fly out of the poem
A vaccine is coming for the poem
How do we ever get the vaccine into the arms of every poem
How do we get poems into everybody's arms

In Praise of Essential Workers

Now we know the value of meat packers
Forced back to work sick
Elbow to elbow. And we are grateful
For delivery men and women double-parked,
Leaping like gazelles from their vans
Dropping packages like gifts on porches,
And truck drivers crisscrossing
The country's highways in thousands of miles
Keeping the lifelines of supplies open
From our farmers harvesting their crops,
And fishermen freezing in the dawn
Icing down their fish in their boats
And store clerks, upbeat, joking through the tedium
Of stocking shelves over and over
And young men running alongside trash trucks
Tossing barrels if they are working out
And mayors and governors
Making the hard decisions
To balance the seesaw of safety and jobs
While nurses and doctors, stressed, exhausted,
Save lives and witness deaths every day
Behind the closed hospital doors.

Just Breathe

Just breathe!
Just breathe till our ambulance gets through this last red light.

Man down.
Blood on the pavement.

We've been told you're a white man
face up; labored breathing.
Age: seventy five.
Just breathe, man.
I'm your paramedic. I'm black.

I know you feel like a rabbit on its back,
legs paralyzed.
Your world is heavy
and black.
You've hit your head on the sidewalk.

Mr. Gugino,
I hope you can hear me.
Your head will be cupped in my open palms
in three minutes, or less.
My hands are gentle and warm,
like a back yard of untroubled tomato plants ripening in the Sun.
My voice is slow
and quiet, a simple breeze off the creek.
I want you to know I love football.
I bet you do too,
so you'll know me
when we meet in a few minutes.
I will touch your body
and ask it a few questions before we head out.

My mother says my voice is slow,
like molasses.
Thick, like honey.
Salty, like those fat pretzels
we get at the game.
She says my voice is a tall glass of lemonade,
a plate of chocolate chip cookies,
that large scoop of vanilla ice cream.

Mom tells her friends at church
every word that comes from her youngest son's mouth is so calm,
like a big raindrop,
a hug from heaven
taking its time to tumble to earth.
Every sentence long and drawn out,
a lazy afternoon summer sun shower.
That slow, wide smile of mine,
a rainbow.

Mom says my hands are rough, but smart, like lawyers.
Clever. Not afraid.
Used to riots in the streets.
Mom used to ask me to get down on my knees
every morning before school
when I was a boy and pray for her.
I kneeled.
Put my hands on the hurt.

Mr. Gugino, do not think about your deceased brother,
your next chemo,
or the marches the two of you went on
for Guantanamo.
Do not think of the dark side of the moon.
In two minutes I'll be at your side.
You'll feel my three fingers curled around your wrist,
and on the pulsing vein under your jaw.

Keeping breathing!
I'm in the back of the ambulance
with you, on my knees,
hands over your heart,
the sirens shrieking
as we race through the last intersection.

Mr. Gugino,
we're going to pretend we're in a huge football stadium,
at the forty yard line.
It's your turn.
The ball's on the turf.
You're going kick that football as high as you can.
We'll watch it sail above the crossbar,
through the goalposts.

Note: All 57 members of the Buffalo Police Department's
Emergency Response Team resigned from the unit after the two
officers were suspended. The unit members did not quit the police
department but stepped down from the tactical unit.

Hospitals Hire Lucifer as Assistant

Hospitals
have hired Lucifer.
Gave him a uniform. An N-95 mask.

He wants to assist when ventilators
have to give up and quit.

At the start of the day,
he reads the long lists
of those who perished.

He calls the living and the non-living,
the ancestors.
Inquires if they want to talk.

The nurses weep
as he delivers large cups of steaming coffee
and rubs rose oil
on their tired ankle bones.

Lucifer is on fire
as he strides the corridors.
Right now, he is on the way to the morgue
to play the bagpipes.

A House of Manifestos

We use the fattest books to smash spiders, then open to page 49 and read. Anything can be bible, but I sleep with the book of *How to Survive Worst Case Scenarios* under my bed, a baggie of drywall screws, and duct tape to hold us together. One article explains that you may feel more scattered than normal, unable to focus. I close my eyes, and see the spread of Northern Lights as hearts taped to neighbor's windows. This too is trauma response. Before she died, my mother made lists on yellow legal pads, so she would not forget how to operate the small machinery of her life. They feathered her cabinets and counters, heavily taped. How many times I've been told that a poem is simply the right words in the right order. I add eye bolts, sifted flour, scissors, salt.

Cross Words

We are two and two in our rectangles
side by side, but 800 miles apart.
If the virus weren't spiking right now,
the two in the other rectangle
would have driven to spend all
the holidays in our rectangular house.
Kid and spouse hoping to come home.

When the host shares his screen,
it's all about the squares.
We each have our own specialties.
One speaks French, one speaks
crosswordese, one speaks techie,
the one who speaks Star Wars,
also speaks Bible. Sometimes
we speak in unison, seeing past
the red herrings to an answer that fits.

It's good to hear these voices.
What a team! And there's never
a cross word among us.

Wonder

I.

In Taiwan, an orange streamer,
massive, tentacles a three-year-old girl.
Her mother strains to anchor her daughter,
but the huge kite lifts high on powerful winds.

The kite yanks the child high in the air.
She rivers through clouds,
a dust mote on a python's tail.
Earth shadows zigzag like strobe lights.

Below, commotion
as the child unfolds from the sky
and waterfalls to earth.
Safe again in her mother's arms.

II.

Every night, this little girl
dreams of birds and clouds.
Her shoulder muscles twitch
and her arms flutter like wings.

She aches to surf wind echoes.
Her eyes are dark with yearning.
She will only wear orange clothes
and she always looks skyward.

III.

In San Francisco, you wake
to your orange cat's unblinking stare.
Trapped behind your front window,
you fold swans from paper squares.

You hunger to fly, long to dream with this child.
Among smoke scrolls and haze,
you search the sky for runes of the child's flight.

Outside the Memory Care Unit During the Pandemic

Press your hand flat against this cold window
match mine – finger to finger, here outside.

Mother,
you inside?

Blue rain falling, turning this gray walkway
into a shimmer of welling wet at my feet.

Meet me palm to palm –
Let's feel the cold barrier warm.
The only magic left us.

Her knobbed fingers push flat
against my calloused ones.

Rain gauzed,
robed in the humid confines of her room,
she stares – milky eyed distraction,
the familiar squint, a new involuntary nodding.
I reach to touch her faded parchment.

I mime her name – *M-oth-er* –
the delicious *m's*, valleyed *o*, gentle growl of the *r*.
mother, mother.

Fish-mouthed, her lips open, close
then stop.
She blinks.
Then steps away.

Two-Sided Pandemic Puzzle

1.

Stay alert, don't walk too close,
zigzag up the street,
honor contagion's choreography.
Have we achieved 8000 steps
to keep our worn joints working?

How long till we must shop again?
Can we cram three weeks' worth
of broccoli, carrots, squash and apples
in our small white refrigerator?

Can this piece of blue soggy cardboard
in the washer be from the Santorini puzzle?
How long till we sit on friends' porches,
play a hand of bridge, attend a live symphony?
How long till we can cruise the world's
cathedrals and museums?

So many hours in the day to fill,
too many missing pieces.

2.

How do I get to work?
Do I pay for gas and parking
or risk infected BART trains?
Will I bring the virus home?

How long till my job disappears?
Can I find another?
How do I juggle rent,
water, electricity, food?

Is 5 a.m. early enough to stand in line
for the bag of pork, rice and beans?
Can my 10-year-old daughter babysit
her 4-year-old brother for 2 hours?
Will I bring the virus home?

Work my job, wipe the car, wash my hands,
care for children and parents,
wash the clothes, wash my hands,
make dinner, wash the dishes,
sterilize surfaces, wash my hands.
Raw with sanitizer, raw with worry.
Have I brought the virus home?

Only 24 hours in a day,
and too many pieces.

Vivace

for Carol

Deaf in one ear, you always sat on my left,
gossiping about Faure's affairs,
praising Schumann's concertos,
as we waited in the silence between sounds.

You taught me how to listen
as the instruments create a universe.
The violins flaunt a phrase,
share it back and forth,
then the cellos commandeer the motif
and weave a counterpoint.
French horns scoop up the notes,
bend and brighten them,
while percussion marks time
till the final crescendo.

You gripped my arm
to signal transcendent parts.
We leaned into melancholy,
held our breaths for menace,
in harmony, released.

With you almost blind now,
confined by the pandemic
to a room too small for your spirit,
we talk by phone. In the background,
Beethoven, Tchaikovsky or Mahler
swells and subsides.
Long after we hang up,
the final notes vibrate and ache.

Blue Arc

Across the sky's holy blue arc,
brushed white clouds fade
to mare's tail whispers.

Cows drowse in the sere yellow fields,
swishing flies with lazy tails.
The dray horse's moist lips linger
over fresh-pitched hay.

Lying beneath this breath-filled expanse,
arms spread, palms up,
my body flattens,
so thin it could sigh
through a window crack.

I could dream for centuries,
and wake to a different world,
heart no longer yoked
to the steel plow.

Permission Slip

Today I permit myself to
forget what I know of gravity,
to awaken inattentive to mass
and weight and feel no force
other than the speed of promise.
I will allow this sensation to
propel me upwards with such
velocity that liftoff will
shake my doubtful features
unrecognizable to the side
of me that seeks to reunite
my bones with Earth.

I wish to remain airborne
as long as possible. I grant
myself permission to stuff
my ears with wind and answer
only to my truest name, to snub
the voices that shout out the
physics and trajectories of me,
that scold "you get down this
very instant, this place is a mess
and soaring time is over."

Looking up after the Storm

I was so
consumed by
the thick bands
of silt that
pulled at
my feet,
I almost
missed
this patch
of light
that is
settling over
the sea.

How What to Wear to a Zoom Class Changed During the Pandemic

The makeup
was the first to go;
my skin thanked me
as it breathed easier.

Many clothes shuttered in my closet
because *Dressed to Impress*
didn't seem to matter anymore,
while books came off my shelves.

(I look smarter now.)

When brown went mousy
and roots to grey,
the hats came out
and onto my frazzled head of hair.

(And I learned a hat can cover up
 a lot of things best hidden.)

After awhile an old t-shirt
and pair of sweats served
as my pandemic uniform.
Then I learned a trick midway –
I could show up
in a bathrobe
if I cut the video.
Remember the make-up
was the first to go.

Now You Know

May 25, 2020
George Floyd, an unarmed black man
gets an instant death sentence
by an officer's knee on his neck

May 26, 2020
Peter Manfredonia, a white man on a killing spree
gets a televised heartfelt plea from a state police officer:
"We know this is not who you are.
Come home and you'll be treated fairly."

It's all there in black and white.
Once you know, you can't unknow.

Now you know.

Haircut Hallelujah

June 16, 2020

I have been sheared
styled
tinted away from despair!
I can now spread my arms wide
shake my shaped tresses
and declare
I am ...
masked, gloved
and six feet away from any
who might care.

Poem Menu

Dear Chula, remember how discussing simple phrases
gave the greatest pleasure – to be "out of sorts" or "beside oneself"
for example, because when did people ever feel "in sorts" or
"inside oneself" or mention when they did? Somehow our echoes,
floating conversations from college days, are helping me
hold the quarantine more kindly. *We're all okay*…but just this moment
how many gasp and die? Who could not feel *out of one's mind?*
While we putter around our cozy homes, staying "safe and sane"
as all the letters finish now, the count ticks up.
Feeling beside myself at every minute? *For you, and you*…
Here's my hope: those surviving will get a menu. A set of memories
"still to think about." An unfinished song. New plans. A group of phrases
folded on a beautiful card, like the "Poem Menus" on hospital trays
in Ireland, the "Poems for Patience" I was asked to pick one year,
all 22 of them, from writers big and small, voices one might wish to meet,
beside the pudding or jello. It was the best job I ever had.
While recovering from surgery or sickness, a patient would find
a surprise toast to Back-to-Life, Slow Time,
succulent words nicely arranged,
and maybe feel their own groggy heads echoing response –
oh, that reminds me of… then something more to think about.
How millions are wishing you all longer lives. Ourselves, as well.
But where is *hither and yon*, for example?
Do they have the virus there?

One

A delivery man pounded the door,
the boy said, *That shook
my bones.*

Only months ago,
before this happened,
on the brink, at the edge –

I kept saying,
*Something really big
and weird is about to happen.*

No one responded, or –
Isn't this weird enough already?
At his father's funeral in Libya,

everyone told Khaled
Aye-zanah-wahad, Our grief is one.
Under the differences, beyond the years

we did not visit. *Wahad. Singular.*
When the sun sinks, we will both
be watching it, perplexed.

I told the boy
I had a bad dream.
He said, *Have a new one.*

Conjuring

A lone exile, I stand at the edge
of this small island and watch the tide
ebb out, flow in.

This water, out of which I'm made,
breeds a froth of discontent.

Searching for whatever lies below and near,
I consult the sand and sift it
through closed fingers like an hourglass.

I hoist clusters of sandy soil
and juggle them like beads –
bright beads, I tell myself,
shining to the farthest star.

I scratch prophecies in dirt,
though I own no knowledge
of the language of the gods,
nor have I tasted their ambrosia.

I invite sea birds, whose circling flight
the priests watch for and interpret,
to pick through scree and from it take
their auspices.

My whole world reduced to sand and ash,
I summon the stars themselves to plummet,
one by one, out of the black sky.

New

Stay inside. Watch how life
starts in secret places. Blossoms lather
in sudsy layers on the bare,
rubbed-raw knuckles and fingers
of the cherry trees. The flycatcher
outside your window sings *whit*
or *clip* or *whee*. Do a tea ceremony
using a clay pot and cylindrical cups.
Savor each sip. Make squash soup
with ginger and be sure to eat it
warm. Feel how it slides into
your belly, dripping light
like the sun. Hear the robin bang
its head against your attic window
thinking its own reflection
is enemy or mate? Don't
do that. Stop. Start with meta-
cognition: this is you.
Not the busyness. The doing.
But listening. Silence. Being.
First preen your feathers,
turning your head this
way and that, admiring
your own reflection. Then fly
into the yard of yourself
and bathe in the stone birdbath,
splashing rainbow drops of water.
Be like the heron: meditate
all day doing your quiet
thing. Or be like the wren: tidy
your home. Clean up messes,
remove layers of dust, and watch

how motes float in ballgowns
of light on the windowsills.
Move your furniture to different
corners, sliding it on rugs.
Create change, but also take into
your hands all things you own
and remember what each
means to your heart. Kiss
the objects your mother
or father used before you,
the curtains your grandmother
crocheted, the cabinets
your great-grandfather carved.
Take family dishes with gold trim
from your shelves and eat
from them instead of saving
them for special days. Read,
make lists of your favorite
words (*testudinate, petrichor, phloem*).
Write poems. Remember
being a child, how every little
moment was instantly holy: fetching
a shuttlecock from the top
of the shed, baking banana bread,
making a drawing for a sick friend.
Remember how much the small
things meant, like growing
sprouts on cotton balls on a chipped
porcelain plate, then eating them
on a cheese sandwich. Pull out
your binoculars. Watch
the Eastern Phoebe spread its tail
over the pond above the slightest waves.
Wake up like spring, like fish
underwater: natural, alone, unafraid.

Tell yourself a new and different
story. Glide for miles like the marsh hawk,
barely flapping your wings. Become
a poem. Laugh the chant of chimes
touched by the hands of the wind.
Then cut out some paper birds
and glue them to your see-through
windows for the next robin
who tries to fly into glass.
Listen to the Barred Owls softly
hooting the night back to light.

Corona Advice from Children

I can't be quiet – my mouth gets itchy
when it has words in it. I want
to get my brain out of my mouth
so silence can bless my throat.
I wish this wasn't real life
and I was just a refrigerator.
I'm going to steal the wings off a bird, fly
up, get you a star, and then give
the bird its wings back. A myth
is a female moth. Is it true that the more
you sneeze, the more blessed you are?
I love the sound of no one talking
or one hand clapping. I can't show you
how much I missed you because
my hands are too small. If you love
people, tell them you love them
as high as the sky. Parmesan cheese
looks like glitter for spaghetti.
If you spill salt or sugar on the table,
the grains scatter like stars.
If you are panicking and feel
like you are dying, take deep
breaths. If you are actually dying, this
won't work. Don't wipe my tears
away. I want to feel them on my face.

This collage poem is composed in part of things said by children as
recorded by teachers or other adults.

How I Live Now

I feel myself slowing
during this stagnant hiatus
when most everything
is closed down, vacant.

I find my body slowing
I sit and sit staring
I grab anything at all
to read including bottles.

I who hate the phone
now pick it up whenever
even make calls to friends
talk for half an hour.

I take my temperature
daily on an old thermo-
meter – uptodate ones
sold out or priced

ten times what they
ought to. One med
already unavailable.
Rich people sent jobs

overseas so finally
little is made here
imports now blocked
supplies exhausted.

We stumble long
half of us vegetating
half maskless spreading
what may kill the rest.

Total Darkness

At the BLM protest, the guy
in a blue truck
with sad-looking American flags
swerves as close to me as he can.
I'm on the sidewalk. All my sign says is
Black Lives Matter.
A friend a few feet away has one
with a Martin Luther King quote.

If he hits me, blood will stain
the flag. I guess he'll feel no grief,
just aim for the next one. It is possible

to be in this world and never see
the sun. Put on a plaid shirt and,
in total darkness, celebrate death.

Manganese Falls

A terrifying beauty
could carry us away.
Leftover autumn leaves
help us relax.
The power we see now
will fade.

In fall, hardly a trickle.

Even a giantess needs
a rest. She dreams
she turns into a spring
torrent – no one
daring to get in her way.

In the Before Times

In the before times, we took dance classes,
not online, but body to body in
a room with a sprung wooden floor. Unmasked,
barefoot and scantily clad in Lycra,
we greeted each other with hugs. Big hugs.
We embraced the drummers, too, if we knew
them, and flashed our unprotected smiles when
the choreography sent us flying
past them. I know it's hard to understand
now, but we didn't worry about rogue
droplets of sweat or aerosolized breath
that might worm their way in and consign us
to horrible illness or death. We thought
only of the wild joy of dancing.

Pandemic Pumpkins

Yesterday I saw the first paddle-like
pale-green leaves of the Cinderella pumpkin
pushed up from the hilly mounds I made
as graves for one of last year's gourds
that went to rot before it could be used.

The English peas I'd planted on top
had come up first,
as delicate as pen-and-ink fairies,
tendrils blindly curling forth to find
support for their climb.

On my hands and knees,
I cleared the ground of weeds –
and added a row, along the fence,
of sunflower seeds.

Though their fruit and flowers
are still months away,
my pumpkins are already
fat and dazzling orange
in the mind's eye,
the sunflowers yellow
against the late-summer sky.

Seeds are hard to come by now;
the sunflowers long past
their use-by date.

But still, any time a dried-up seed
manages to germinate and grow,
flower and thrive, it's truly a miracle.
Who's to say a seed won't wait
three years or even ten?

Seed banks count on some of them
possessing the biological patience
to stay viable, on pause,
till they're embraced by dirt again,
licked to life by water,
and awakened from enchanted sleep
by sunlight and heat.

I'm witness to this resurrection
every day of my gardening season.
How can I not believe
that life will triumph
over lockdown and decay?

Dear

The world has a blue mask,
I live in its caves.
Only my footprints
are visible.

I was born
with a mask on,
they don't know me
from a deer.

Nothing But A Dream

Try to grasp the dream
and it's always one door beyond.
You're reaching for the handle
moments too late.
A billowy door blows shut,
cloth of the dream.

Looking Through a Window into Someone Else's Life

It's a very bitter day.
If you pass away today on a bright sunny day
it would be a good day
to enter the hearts of those you love.

If you pass away tomorrow on a cloudy rainy day
it would be a good day
to become spirit and soul
and enter the hearts of those you love.

Time has no meaning. Roots of my biggest pine
rise up through the earth like fingers
reaching to pull you back.

Ashes of the Fallen

Feather, fur, blood and bone
hang in the violent sky.
Delicate, drifting funerals
anoint my windshield.

California, a grave now,
mourns beneath the charred
remains of a thousand souls.

I gather ashes of Coyote, Deer, Rabbit, Mouse
and piece them back together.
I weep blessings
and send them on their star journey.

My Appointment with Worry

This week is long,
and I must return home
for my appointment with worry.

Worry is part mother,
part exposure to danger.
Worry exists because
I feed her. At the coffee shop
I treat her to coffee and scones.
We're at peace for a few minutes before the next assault.

Worry doesn't care about details,
but she gossips like a yenta.
She knows what lives in my veins,
the adrenalin rush of a fallen rock garden.

Nights are the hardest. The wind
forces itself through the valves
of my heart. I read about the man in Vegas,
where the constant cries of wind traveled indoors
to his brain. He went insane, anxieties
adhered to his nerve endings.

I take worry on a field trip,
open the back door of the library
and enter a wind tunnel. Glossy sounds
vibrate through the pipes overhead –
a chamber of crystalline chandelier.

Worry says I see sounds as colors
and finds these sounds disturbing.
Worry studies her watch.
She can't leave fast enough.

Worry says, forgive Memory.
Memory goes out into the world
and enjoys a glass of wine
while her date enjoys 4 martinis.
Then she looks up
and it's four hours later.

After dinner we sit across from each other.
I guide worry through the seven chakras.
She wants to reel in the calm
for future reference.
Her forehead softens,
her temples at peace.

Worry is aware of her face.
She plaits her hair, looks beautiful
so that she can attract me like a new dress.

We hold hands and play patty cake.
We hold hands and our fingers drift apart
as a strange sensation moves up my arm.

Worry supports me in ways I hadn't noticed.
Without her, I wouldn't have left early
to get that parking spot.

Without worry, I wouldn't have looked
3 times before crossing the street.
Worry asks, Do you believe in ghosts?
More than ever, I say as I pace.

Memory is watching.
Days flip like a flip book
and I don't remember which day
happened first, or in which year;

maybe I remember things
that never happened.

The next afternoon Memory stops by
and says we must meditate on impermanence.
Memory has gaps but she keeps
retelling the same story,
hoping to find her way.

When worry returns, I make everyone tea
while I pack for the airport.
Even with plane delays, time changes, and one lost iPhone,
Worry is waiting for me when I arrive.

Puzzles During Quarantine

In quarantine, we
turn to jigsaw puzzles: take pleasure in
the firm but gentle snap when pieces join.
I daydream I'm at the lake on that red bench,
or climbing the cliff, not realizing an old man
is already at the top.

I work my way through watery domains:
lakes, coves, estuary,
then switch to woodland terrains.

The only thing to do is surrender
to the bamboo forest
I am piecing together, to set one foot
toward the umbrella pine
and keep my hands from shaking,
my emotions from plummeting,
and puzzle this afternoon
to numb the gnawing pain.

With nowhere else to look
for the future, I focus
on finding the last piece
of this sun.

Finding the Heartbeat in a Church Garden

The theologian guides us to a contemplative break,
invites each of us to go outside,
see the face of God in what we find.
He says, "There is a heartbeat to the divine. Listen."

Do I close my eyes to go within?
I sit on stone near a sunlit tree
beside St. Francis cradling a deer.
I close my eyes but miss the glisten
of the tree. Under shafts of sunlight
how do I listen to the voice of branches,
whispering sky, the sacred in what is lit alive,
the subtle song of morning?

He says our minds are like a tree
with monkeys swinging from the branches.
Or maybe he says screaming. I cannot tell.
And my mind is like that ringing bell that calls us back.
Either way, I agree. So many monkeys in the tree
including the favorite brooch I lost somewhere
on my way here today. I place my hand on my heart, pray
and try again to listen.

Tanka

the shadow
of a long-sleeved Buddha
reaches still
for the porcelain vase
my heart flowers

Virtual Amateur Chorus

The woman with her mouth
shaped in a perfect "O"
I imagine she sings opera
or is in a fine classical chorus.
I see Ellen in her
Zoom's square living room,
the daughter of an old friend's friend
from Berkeley. The conductor is in
his home country of Sweden.
It is eleven a.m. in San Francisco.
It is night in Sweden,
but I can see through his window pine trees
and it is still light out.
From eleven to twelve,
I do not check virus numbers
or watch the news.
In our hundreds of soundless little spaces,
the harmony, unheard, is perfect.

White Garden-i-a

White Garden-i-a
Shines through dark air, filled with ash
Giving love and hope

Isolating in the Pandemic

From your little island in the neighborhood
you have levitated into the unlit realms of time.

The terror of infinity and the moment is all you have
isolated in your small island home.

It's like jumping off into the void
the past is full of life, the future is now.

In the ocean of space the moment
grows, increases in larger circles.

The substantial earth is no more, the unadorned soul
discovers herself in the world of the eternal.

Before the Wildfires

She wrote the phone number
hastily on the palm of her hand.
Rode home hard and fast on her lucky bike.
The number partially disappeared
with the hot sweat of her palm.

She dashed into the house
copied the number on a grocery receipt.
Wind began to bang against the house,
warning trees and power lines could be down
in the coming days.

Her lights flickered
the living room lost electricity.
Under the last low light
she looked at the number again.
She wanted to think
about the phone number
alone in the dark.

Lentil Soup

When I make my special lentil soup
the scent of garlic
flows throughout the house, steam rising.
The hardy soup cooked to perfection
lentils savory in a bowl from Greece or Saudi Arabia.

Best of all the vegetables, carrots, celery,
onions compliment each other
sautéed in butter, garlic and black pepper.

A thick piece of crusty bread
sliced with a knife, a wedge of sharp cheddar
all swallowed down
with a glass of cold white wine.

In a short while I'll go up to bed
fall into the down comforter,
beneath flannel sheets, satisfied.
Contentment arrives in the night.

A Turn Toward Red

Cherries burn in their green nests
windows to a red world

Tiny finches steal them and so do we
a wilderness of bees in the garden

Flesh rose, guilder rose, hawthorn
and holly, the cardinal's racket

Red tide, the color of deep adobe
rolls relentlessly toward shore

Red weather in the heart

Unhindered red
a quick bright tongue lick

Unending flow of red
in blood we came

In blood we will go
a scaffold of stone

Crimson center of coronavirus
being here is everything

For All That Is Lost

It's easy to love forgotten fields,
pathless woods, empty lots.

I will be a scavenger of life
in a new wilderness.

I embrace the misplaced beauty
of overgrown ditches –
nettles, thistles, blackthorn.

Praise no man's land –
plastic bags, broken bottles,
gulls feeding on garbage,

fish near sewage pipes, bear
lurking near the dump, pathogens
freed to kill us

while on the edges, ravens
try over and over
their broken notes.

In a Time of Distancing

For Tim

Sometimes I just want to touch you
when I'm caught in the honeyed notes of the cello,
or hearing the chorus of gulls quarrel
at low-tide feast, the drumming of surf
in their throats.

I live in the silence between notes
between whistle-cries of the finches,
in the caesura of being present.

The world wants to be loved.
Andrea Bocelli sings for us
in the hollow glitter of Milan Cathedral.

On the steps in front of soaring doors
and statues of the saved,
he sings, "I was blind but now I see,"

while videos of cities without people flash onscreen –
the Seine with no bookstalls,
Trafalgar with no traffic,
Times Square, a crazy tunnel echoing
the in-your-face circus it was.

The space between Tibetan bowl moon
and undulating sheet of sea buzzes with ions.
In the opera of what we're living through,
you help me stay grounded when stars call.
I touch you in the spaces of my longing.

The Pandemic Has Taken the Writer's Coffeehouse

but it hasn't yet pilfered my imagination! Is that
the aroma of coffee roasting? Am I virtually
stepping in – are the floorboards creaking under my feet
just like always? Ah, there are the pastries in the glass case.
There's nothing to stop me from choosing the one with
apple filling. No. Make that blueberry. In my hand
the old-fashioned white cup. I wait my turn to
pour in a heavy dose of cream, then hold the chalice –
oh paradise – under the spigot and open
the flood gates for Guatemalan Dark Roast.
I'm navigating to my spot. I'm placing my treasures
upon my table. Here I am in my coffeehouse with a
dozen of my best strangers. I fish the notebook
out of my backpack, lay it at the
ready; I'm geared up. After all those losses,
not all is lost. Soon I will write such drivel as
the world has never seen. First a well-deserved
pastry, the soft brown crust, the warm fruit,
hot sips of nirvana, then I give myself the whole
morning to write across page after page after page.

For the Asking

Ask a priest or the moon what whispers past the night sky
Ask children or sparrows what blackberries taste like
Ask babies or cats why they pummel soft objects

Ask ICU nurses or doves how to mourn complete strangers
Ask mosquitoes or sadists the purpose of torment
Ask generals or snakes how it feels to cause pain
Ask liars or red maples where to drip sticky sweetness

When they offer their answers, arrange them
in a box lined with stars, silver tears and soft wool,
and leave it out for the dustman's collection of dreams.

Return of the Golden-Crowned Sparrows

I call the golden-crowned sparrows,
and one, two, three, four,
they flutter down and light
on the stone lip of the fountain
to play in the falling stream,
washing from wings and throats
the dust of their long journey,
the ash of wildfires,
sending up a blaze of droplets
in the October sun.

They answer me with a clear whistle,
three equal notes descending,
do ti so.
We are here, they seem to say.
We have returned, even though
the hills are still burning.
We have seen from the sky
the flash of water,
a glint in earth's eye promising rest,
and we have come back again.

Kneading the Challah

I push, fold, and turn the dough
until the heels of my palms complain.
Now is the time to pray.

I think of my daughter,
fighting so hard to live into her gifts.
I think of my great-great-grandmothers,

nameless, tireless, eternal,
braiding prayers for their own daughters
into their golden loaves.

I think of the families broken by this cruel pandemic.
I think of our planet healing in this immense pause,
of how the earth might teach us to live another way.

Brimming with a wordless, empathic longing,
I grope toward intention. At that very moment,
a voice comes over the kitchen radio,

singing of light and of promise,
singing of compassion and of strength.
I am too near tears to sing along,

but the dough smooths under my aching hands,
and my own prayer takes shape and begins to rise
like the oiled round in the big red bowl–

a prayer for this beautiful world.

Inspired by Kathy Kallick's song, "This Beautiful World"

Praise in Dark Times

Praise the sorrow that took us out in the night –
the cold snap of wind in her sails
Praise the king tides that spilled us
        onto the shore of this difficult day

Praise the mystery that rises when the ground gives way
Praise the toppling of arrogant men cast in bronze
Praise the night and what we cannot see
        Praise all that is dark

Praise the black boys and girls
with hearts as big as Africa
Bless their soul-deep eyes
and the songs the earth gave them
in secret   to sing

Bless their singing as it enters us
Bless the singing earth as she enters us
Bless the sacred songs
        in all the forgotten keys

Day of Distancing

Enter the ways of morning, the body
of morning – the waking of bee and leaf,
spider and newt. The way morning sun catches
in the threads that shuttle thoughts
between the trees, visible only in this light.

Have you noticed how, when we finally let go,
all we've ever wanted comes?
By which I mean love – not the come-and-go,
flare-and-fade kind, but love as a cloud of gnats
you can walk through, or as the kingfisher's
impossible stillness on his branch above the lake.

How did we come to think we had no time for this?

These days seem mostly to give us ourselves,
over and over … happy to take us, to break us open –
wider, deeper and more true.

My grandsons want to visit – all 4 of them, strong
and singular as the four directions. And my sable-skinned
granddaughter – queen of the night. I want
to take each one in my arms. *Oh, what the hell,*
I say when no one is listening, *let me die of hugging.*

But instead I stay inside and hold them
here – distanced and masked.

Most things are smaller now, except for what's big –
like when our hearts break each day and set loose
the strands the weavers will use in the night –
threading them at lake's edge to catch the morning light.

How to Befriend Uncertainty

Come sit in the seat by the window –
near the birds who have shaken off
their dreams and opened themselves
to this never-to-be-again day.

Today we won't be asked
to bumble along the beaten byways,
for Uncertainty is our houseguest.
Put on the water,
set out the homemade jam.

Uncertainty will listen with us
as our bagels pop
from the toaster's dark mouth
and the coffee grounds weep
their bittersweet sobs.

Uncertainty is Mystery's love child –
no history, no proper name –
but she has always been with us.

She is the one who wakes us
to drizzle new questions into our day,
new stories, new colors and light.

The wind is her breath.
Her body is the water
we bathe in and drink.

Uncertainty, with her
barefoot-dancing gypsy soul
knows the unpaved roads
to gratitude by heart.

But of certain things – like tomorrow –
she knows nothing.

And because of this,
her love knows no bounds.

Quarantine Cleaning

Like an archaeologist,
I sift through the strata of my life
while excavating filing cabinets

My history emerges:
6th grade report card, 9th grade writing folder,
college papers, and master's thesis
Job applications and resumes
with changing addresses and interests
Writing samples and grants I'd forgotten doing
My face staring back at me from newspaper clippings
Effusive evaluations and thank you notes
from students declaring a competency I never felt
Poems from my high school boyfriend
and later lovers. Cards sent to me
showing how much I was loved,
words flowing from people now buried
Invitations to my once-famous garlic parties
Pictures of people who used to be my friends,
some I no longer recognize
Lists of things I meant to read or watch,
of words I meant to write with
And unremembered words I'd written
Pain exposed by pen only to be hidden
in unmarked file folders

Fragments of who I used to be
dug up, dusted off, neatly labeled
then filed away again

Stones for the Dead

– a reflection on George Floyd

A stone is placed on his neck,
just at the point where his spine
holds his head upright.
But he is on the ground, face in the dirt,
like so many before him.
Hot asphalt and the grit of sand
left by tires and boots
cradle his cheek. In pain,
he finds his mother
caressing his head, her tears
washing the stain of death
from his closed eyes.

He is borne away on the river
where the boatman lays
his broken body, now ready
to rise.

Pandemic Puzzle

Thin clouds stretch overhead, striations
pulled taut by fear. I touch edges worn out
by the drip of dis-ease.

Nothing fits these days. Paths meander
in woods still bare from winter. Spring
refuses to stay in a world empty of hope.

Yet the daily pattern emerges, even
in dreams heavy with anxiety. Who will die?

I hike every day to feel the ground sturdy
beneath my boots, to hear phoebes greet me
with their two-note hello, to know
that I am not needed in this landscape.

I look into the mirror of the lake
as dawn spreads and see
only the wisp of clouds across the sky.

Surrender

I cradle my head into the smallest of arms
⅛ of my size & still I melt like butter on a
morning pan. Digging into my hair; his fingers exploring each strand
like a treasure each sound I make his heartbeat jumps a beat quicker.

Here I surrender; a piece of driftwood on a river a distant
nursery rhyme shouts in the bedroom another toy I forgot to shut off.

He rubs my forehead as if I was a genie in a lamp &
he asks for nothing in return other than this time
together.

Guardian of Sound

Harmony is your birthright –
listen for the perfect pitch within.
Ancestors' whispers gently nudge you,
whoosh of wings. Birds rise through
pine tree's hiss, as the breeze trills a chorus of frogs
and the murky pond ripples.

Each time you embrace one another,
cascades of pure light shine
through the dissonance.
It takes less than you know,
but you've grown deaf to silence,
and the hum of pure being.

The rake and hoe of light and darkness
reap the seeds you sow.
Violent outbursts batter and threaten existence,
as the backwash sucks and pulls apart
your true nature.

When discord tips the eternal balance,
I pluck a chord.
Lovers of beauty offer memory
teachers and healers,
reach those who listen
as dissonance dissolves.

Crystal threads of light and sound
entwine the fabric of the universe.
I move through energy
sleight of hand long forgotten.
I am the mirror.

Pure energy like shimmered heat
off desert pavement
merges, separates, pulses vibration.
I am the guardian of sound
ancestor to no one, ancestor to all.

On the Death of John Prine

It's been years since the woman I've become
has heard you sing, but I'm sitting in a house
of wood among oak trees remembering that voice
of yours as it once carved deep streams among
the rocks we traversed, backpacks on our shoulders
our three kids upfront or trailing behind, and the small
Sierra towns we'd driven through into the California
backcountry, dog wagging her tail in someone's
face, or on our yearly trek to the Trinity River, always
in the presence of your gravelly tones, keen eye, perfect
listening ear, riotous humor, a bowl of oatmeal staring
you down, you'd twang, or you'd tell us about losing
Davy in the Korean War, *O, Hello in There,* John Prine,
I can't eat a peach without the words of your *Spanish
Pipedream* coming in through my teeth with the taste,
the juice, and those instructions of yours "Blow up yore TV"
rocked my mind today when I heard you'd gone down into
our national outrage, our huge Covid19 annals where
the truest American voice I've ever heard had just expired...

You Walk Barefoot into Yourself, Lit by Love into the World

Between moonshine and sunshine
rest good moments. Between evenings
when raccoons
pull down hummingbird feeders
and days of conference
calls in pajamas, you go clumsy, drop your laptop
into a fantasy where someone else picks it up,
hands it to you without fear of touching.
Now your colleagues wonder where you've gone,
and you say you're still here.
But you're out asking the moths
how they feel today, touching their soft bodies
to your face, that strange, now seldom-touched
planet. You're out opening doors
for a new communion, opening your hand
to anything willing to land in it.

Quarantine Bingo

Attended Zoom Meeting in Work Shirt & Underwear	Hoarded Anything	Broke Down For No Apparent Reason in Public, Looked Longingly at Strangers Who Could Not Hug You for Comfort	Got Mad at Someone Else for Hoarding Anything	Thought You Had Covid-19 Didn't Have Covid-19 Had Covid-19 Didn't Have Covid-19
Celebrated Birthday on Zoom with Virtual Cake	Paid People for Services They Are No Longer Able to Perform	Stayed in Bed for an Entire Day, Calling Everyone You Know to See if They Were Still Alive But Pretended you Were Just Calling to Say Hi	Home-schooled Your Children While Drinking a Martini	Gave a Non-Mask Wearer the Stink-eye, Dramatically Stepped Two More Feet Away
Took Covid Test in Your Car	Installed Wet Bar in Your Workspace	FREE for ESSENTIAL WORKERS	Used Curbside Cannabis Pick-Up	Extra Free Space / You Deserve It
Received Payment for Services You Can No Longer Perform	Wiped Your Face With a Clorox Wipe, Realized It, Freaked Out, Rinsed Clorox off With Water	Watched as Someone Else Broke Down For No Apparent Reason in Public, Looking Longingly at You and Other Strangers Who Could Not Hug Them for Comfort	Organized All Drawers and Closets While Drinking a Martini	Pulled Yourself Successfully From the Lake of Tears You Were Drowning In
Put Medicine on Your Geriatric Cat's Butt With Saran Wrap Around Your Finger Because You Couldn't Get Gloves	Hung Your Mask on the Rear-View Mirror Next to Religious Icon, Mardi Gras Beads, Or Graduation Tassels	Extra Free Space / You Deserve It For Not Running Naked Through the Street Smoking the Stale Cigarette You Got From the Pack You Saved When You Quit Six Years Ago	Baked Bread or Made Cookies. Did or Did Not Include Butter from Curbside Cannabis Pick Up	Looked at Coronavirus Worldometer More Than Ten Times in One Day, Made Martini

For the Past Month, I've Felt Like
Andy Warhol's Silver Clouds

Intangible. Floating. So, the day after Easter, I visit the Tate Modern's
Warhol Exhibit online. Life is its own factory. I dream of drag queens

and torsos, Marilyn Monroe and condensed tomato soup. In the future,
everyone will be famous for fifteen minutes. But who counts among

everyone? Which tweet will come wading out of the whirlpool of ennui
with its daydream in its hand? The retweets too are a daydream. Like love

in an elevator that only goes up. Like fifteen new moons to orbit you.
The mind too is a factory. Churning out what we train it to make.

Today, I will read the news only once. And then I will cultivate: art,
beauty, hope, a cloud-footed dancer spinning out of a silver dream.

Let's

after Prartho Sereno

Let's hang sheets of rain on a clothesline,
dangle lavender bundles from curtain rods,
carry bars of soap in our pockets
to scrub the stricken air.

Let's pull up weeds and plant them
in places they won't recognize.

Bring hummingbirds inside
to hover in our living rooms.

Let beetles burrow through memories
to get to the bottom of things.

Our minds are too much on hold.

Let's free them to slip
by that ominous cloud,

and patchwork a quilt
of front porch stories
that make no sense
to the fearful heart.

Taking a Knee

Martin Luther King
going down at Pettus Bridge.
Colin Kaepernick going down
during the national anthem.

Now a policeman goes down
beside a protester
because George Floyd
and others like him are dead.

Ending racism is a bridge to be crossed –
a connection to the other side,
a point of moving forward.

Like Jesus when he knelt
at Gethsemane,
where he prayed for himself,
where he prayed for us.

Necessary Trouble

In memory of John Lewis

I admit it. So many of my troubles
are optional, self-created, even
absurd. I have borrowed trouble
too many times to count, even
when no one offered to loan it.
I've made work from laziness
and embarrassment out of inattention.
I have chosen to be clever
rather than kind, and Lord knows
irritable when what was needed
was some measure of grace.
Don't even get me started
on the unnecessary troubles
wished on us by those
who've chosen division
over the more perfect union
we were promised.
There isn't time.
The walls, it seems, are closing in.
There is only time for
necessary trouble, as in
God's gonna trouble the waters.
As in, the tide is rising
and we're going to need
a bigger boat.

These Days

Anyone who tells you not to be afraid
should have their head examined.
Cities are burning, hillsides are burning,
and the dumpster fire of our common life
is out of control. I wish I could tell you
when it was going to get better.
I wish I could promise that *better*
was anywhere down this road.
I miss dancing, bodies in something
between conversation and flight.
I miss singing, the way we trusted
the air that moved between us. I miss
the casual assumption that everything
would be alright in the morning.
These days I am trying to be buoyed
by the smallest things –
a ripe tomato, a smattering of rain.
These days I am trying to remember
that songs of lamentation
are still songs.

May I Tell You?

I want to tell you this,
purged of pretense,
clear as the stars opening their white eyes
in this February mid-winter sky
after the storm has swept away
every turgid cloud
just the pure, naked expanse of black,
silver-glittered, saying
"Begin new."
                    If you have breath
there's time yet to find a different way.
Put on the stars' radiant shawl.
Don't be afraid to shine.

Again

Last night's food riots in my stomach
as I watch millions of eyes watch
a black man's life end in the street –
the weight of a knee on his neck
          for eight minutes.
The *Blue* pressing his knee listens,
hands in his pockets, to the bound man
cry out for his mother.
His mother's grave cries.
His brother pleads,
"My family wants peace."

After his lifted knee, did the officer go home
make a peanut butter and jelly sandwich, kiss his wife,
wash guilt from his hands?

Pain, that strong current, rips through the world,
its waves crushing as massive stones.
Descendants, non-descendants of slaves are feathers
on injustice's cruel bird.
Unrest dirties the night with orange flames –
anger mumbles through crowds
mixed with mourners and mutineers.
Why does innocence draw disgrace?
Can spirits rust?
Who can place a curfew on despair?
What saw can slice a wall of indifference?

A trio of *Blues* refuses to serve and protect
another black man.
Their silence – his death.

Will We Desire Touch?

After the COVID-19 kryptonite
is discovered, will we desire touch –
that primitive longing
swaddled in our lives before birth?
Will it be more desirable
than clasping light between our teeth
in a world darkening with dread?

Before this phantom smuggled
panic into our lives,
beliefs broke friendships,
family relationships,
kind words became crushed bricks,
crumbled from the weight
of anger's battering.

Curious how this fear forces wide
        the circle of distance,
how the invisible separates us.

And those souls who depend on a stranger's touch
for comfort: a brush of fingertips from the grocery clerk,
a bump from the waitress burdened with too many trays,
a pat on the back from the worker at a soup kitchen,
the volunteer who rocks an orphaned child
in the neonatal intensive-care unit.
Is there a surrogate for the warm arch of flesh?

Oh! To fill air and lungs, lives and loneliness
with the dust of crushed kind words.
Let their film cover computer,
telephone, television screens.
Let their residue stick to hands flush against glass

as they reach for companionship from the pit of isolation.
And for those whose hands cannot reach
beyond cardboard boxes, may they hear
friendly voices echoing from heart-to-heart
in this dark season of distancing.

Ode to Cracker Jacks

Giddy as a child, I tear the cellophane wrapper's grip
from the *Things I Ate as a Kid* 1,000-piece puzzle box.
I read the name of each snack, drink, boxed meal, smile
at the ones I can still get from a grocery shelf.
A hodgepodge of flavors competes for a space on the cover –
the salty crunch of Fritos, sweet cold of Popsicles,
carbonated fizz of Bubble Up.
A blizzard of colorful cardboard falls
as I pour pieces onto tagboard,
each shape different as fingerprints.

I sift through the pile in search of edges,
cluster like colors, find an eye among the pinks,
mustache in the blues, nose among the whites.
Isn't this the way we shape our being, framing edges,
clustering, sifting through partial pieces to make a whole?
Isn't this the beauty of time, to connect each vine of thought,
plan, dream as we watch our lives form?

My hands carry me back to that happy place
where I climbed trees, played with tea sets, made mud pies
as I lock matching pieces together, rejoice when
Cracker Jacks, Wonder Bread, CHEEZ-IT,
Fiddle Faddle, Captain Crunch, Kool-Aid are complete.
A flame of need for a moment in my past burns in me –
age ten, I run up and down Carver Street screaming with laughter
until the sky drains itself of blue.
The past is a wet wick I cannot ignite;
I walk to the pantry get a bag of CHEEZ-IT –
my tongue cannot tell the difference between then and now.

East Jesus

Now that I can't travel, I have a hankering
for East Jesus, south of the Salton Sea, a place
that's said to boast a transient cast of artists,
builders, writers, musicians, freethinkers,
merry pranksters, wandering messiahs,
the dispossessed, and the damned.

No travel brochures. A place to enjoy
from a distance, in the mind, free
of the unfortunate encumbrances
of physical activity in the desert,
surrounded by dust and stinking
port-a-lets and dirty humans who think
they know the will of God or enjoy
making dioramas out of industrial waste
or think they can build the New Jerusalem
out of castoff TVs. Still, as a place in the mind,

I'm making room for East Jesus and wondering
about the suburbs, East of East Jesus and Far West
East Jesus and the distant neighboring community
of Beelzebub, to the south, which scorns messiahs
and favors those who think they are accursed
but know how to build air-conditioners and make
delicious mixed drinks. East Jesus: my travel fantasy.

So attractive, now that I know I can't go.
Maybe my neighborhood has emigrants. You know,
the usual: the dispossessed, the damned.

How to Dress Like You Have Someplace to Go

No need to dwell on your imagined destination.
Rule out of course the Himalayas and the Taj Mahal.
Decline a private audience with the Pope. Bypass
that special fete at the Kennedy Center celebrating
you and you alone. Start small: a visit that requires
underwear. Build from there: Levis will get you
most of the places you want to go. An oxford shirt
gives you the look of a collegiate personality.
Tie shoes, of course, will let you walk the walk.
As for the rest, you can shine it on. Speak
the language of the literate, and don't forget
to shave. Then sit down in silence and think
of all the places you're happy you don't need to go.

Shelter

PBS NewsHour, April 19, 2020

Animal shelters emptying as our houses
fill. A young girl and mother in NYC

grabbed a Calico named Hillie
nosing her litter, five of them,

one hot in the girl's palm which helps
the way heat on a bruise helps.

When there's so much to heal we rely
on the smallest of hearts, knocking its

rapid pulse in a cupped hand as if panicked
though deep in a non-pandemic sleep.

The girl's face rapturous, quiet.
Shelter keeps surprising me with its two faces

the one stifles, the other saves – and its many
guises, like a garden stumbled into around a bend.

Out in the city, sirens. A world we reel from
each night and can't recognize come morning,

fodder for a virus leaping into the human sea
as we dive into the ocean because it's there

and we can, without thought or purpose
but to live another day. Shelter

the opposite of wander, a place to pause
protected, as by a shield. In an apartment

in NYC a mother and daughter.
Hardwood floors. Kitties

slip-sprawling to mama's teats,
eyes closed for the moment.

Spread

March 2020

Then a breeze came
and it wasn't safe to laugh

on porches, I couldn't
extend my hand

future vague as a sideways
thought, as the distant haul-trucks

on I-5, their bulk a strange
presentiment of hidden cargo.

As long as rain washes the low
hills wrapped in their

green pelt this late March,
we delude ourselves that

swiftness isn't the way
of life, desperation

won't overtake the blistering
hours. Life through a window pane

dread of insidious guests
silent as a powder puff

chalking my face
that residue we laughed off

in ordinary times. Alarm comes
nightly now and unfailing.

Quarantine Days

Grab me my lap-
top honey I want to
Google that map
of penitence you
told me about yes
let us chart a course
of survival through
all of these our wrongs
O all around us the stakes
are high (Here dwells the proud
virus insolent as Zeus all pulse &
aggravated muscularity, a panther
stalking its prey) while through
the jungle shadow of apartment
halls nobody knows what steps
to take it's leap son leap whose
neck is getting snapped today
on a street corner or in a subway
train, hiding in the winecellar
among the corks (we are the
littlefish now) ladies & gents
bottom of the foodchain
a wading bird called death
is about to pluck some of us
up & it could be me or you
(a bolt of lightning in the
sweet sweet shallows where
we have swum, undisturbed)
steady, steady, sunlight breaking
through a window curtain
the winter clouds part, sky
is heading due north, a blue

crocus fists its way through
parking lot concrete, audacious!
(All day long in a white & purple
robe zombie Spring moves feebly
thru the empty streets) O ruins of
Babylonia no intermediary or
biblical heaven between us &
the happy strangler not even
Athena Queen of the air can do
much to protect us though everything
else she touches turns to gold (O
Athena of the mad & driven
rain, O the baked clay &
mud flats beckon with
prehistoric tides) what
seas are these how
they rise they fall
mother, like horizons
yielding to the inevitable
sun (I offer no solace) –
a flock of migrating birds
crosses the Kansas
plains, they are headed
for Minnesota & the long
gone tall grass prairie – what
memory earth possesses!
& what exactly are we to earth,
sharp hooves, thundering
herds – we are the intruders,
imposter gods, sheltering in,
wondering what we got when
we traded our souls in, our holy
original animal nature for broad
commerce & civilization (& do
not forget) it is us who disturbed

the universe turned it all upside
down (yes & our mien to live
unmeasured lives & overstep
boundaries) but see how,
across Fifth Ave. a lone coyote
trots, songbirds invade
Rockefeller Plaza, all
is well, Central Park is
a gathering pool of
sullen water, raccoons
crawl out of manhole covers
& it is all a new day
for the rest of nature,
a stimulus package
for the bumblebees,
(but who is this woman
braiding her long black hair
over on the other side, what nativity I
so much desire! where the riverbank
meets the sky) & in the algebra of
these quarantined days, a century
passes, unnoticed (O one more fling
at it peoples!) & well may we return
& well punished for our excesses,
& put in our place.

(A continent wide
morning song's
pouring like blue
birds out of heaven,
into the Chesapeake,
into the North Atlantic,
into the Gulf of Mexico)

I Dream of Apple Blossoms and Young Fruit

I dream of apple blossoms and young fruit, and songbirds that
      fall silent,
and a death toll mounting, some of them six days dead and
      waiting on gurneys;

I dream of cop cars colliding in sunlight and rain, of ambulances
      in heavy wind
and hail, and down by the harbor a bolt of lightning splitting
      the sky and an angry
seagod thrusting himself out of green seawater again and again
      (out he comes, grinning);

I dream of seagulls scattered and innocents caught like deer in
      the fever's spell,
and in the front garden a veil of purple and white renegades,
      magnolia petals falling;

And on the radio the terrible news, I hear the dead and dying
      all around me, 799 dead
in NY State in one day alone, that was yesterday and no dream;

And the magnolia petals too radiant for words or witnessing,
      and the quarantined living
too flush with fear and boredom of waiting to sing or to pray;

And in the aftermath of spring's unexpected squall whole
      clusters of flowers still clinging
to the branch, trembling above the littered dead;

Sunshine and rain, little to savor, only the taste of earth mixed
      with rainwater;

Little to soothe the throat or tongue, this in the year of our
       plague April 9th, 2020,
this parachute of death, as grief comes to us with no
       instructions, as songbirds go
silent and the sly fox huddling in the low shrub;

And as there is no way to mourn or to roll back the rock; and as
       there is no way
to ask the stars to keep their distance, or heaven to offer
       explanations;

And as there is no time to count the days calmly or
       contemplate or reason away
this provocation, only to bite down hard on the bitter pill, pour
       fever into a cup
and drink it down;

O! open up the vaults of heaven whoever you are!

Our morgues are full, we have dug all the trenches on all the
       islands of the world
to hold them, they are just filling up too fast, even the armies of
       Jesus could not
hold them all;

O! as heaven is residence to you and our prayers, we call upon
       you in heaven,
whoever you are! Try to understand, help us to wheel them
       down the long corridor,
our dead must make way for the not yet dead (to be planted
       where? in your funerary
sky, give them temporary rest in your graves among the stars);

We ask this small thing, it is only temporary, we will come for
      them at some future
undetermined date, that's a promise; like minerals on the moon,
      we will dig them up
and remember them and reinter their remains according to our
      custom and leave you
to your own transactions;

Meanwhile let them reside among you and your stars, our
      orchard of the dead;
To flower like renegade magnolia blossoms;
To flourish in perfect little imperfect rows;
To fall, as white apple blossoms fall in spring;
And to bear in heaven what heavy fruit they may.

Yellow Moon Gone Pink

New York Harbor, dark waters, the Great White Way is shuttered now, Fifth Avenue's a drag strip for cop cars and emergency vehicles, and a big damn moon is rising like a single daffodil over the city, hangman moon, like an innocent bird of prey

And the ships roll in
And the ships roll out

Except for one ship that's parked off shore by the Verrazano Bridge

Waiting for the all clear sign
Waiting for the gangplank to roll
And sweet release from the quarantine ship

Don't be afraid of each other or yourselves, people! The invisible invitation to die has already landed and spread across America.

Safe Harbor? No harbor is safe! Never was, never will be. Release the passengers of the good ship plague, this town has seen it all before

Small Pox Yellow Fever Black Death Spanish Flu Polio Plague – all landed here

Covid 19, same old story

The ships roll in, the ships roll out – from Liverpool Bremerhaven Wuhan Yokohama Port au Prince – cargo ships, cruise ships, tugs and tankers and barges too; cars refrigerators palm oil crude oil bananas and grapefruit and sand. And women and men – social climbers, grifters, uptight, chill; undiscovered and overrated; the talented and the decrepit and the young. And plenty of illegal whiskey.

Stowaways too, and rich Americans with private cabins and
obscene spending money.

Piraeus Le Havre Denmark Italy Holland Portugal South
America Spain. All the same –
And the jumbo jets, pregnant with hope and money and death,
flying in over rooftops and tenement buildings, from here to
Far Rockaway

And the oil refineries in New Jersey.
And the sugar refineries in Brooklyn.
And the power plants along the East River.
And the water towers and interstates.

And the hallways ringing with the ghosts of centuries, other
generations of quarantine, soup in the kitchen, radiators
banging and wet socks; and the crying and laughter of the ones
who made it, or didn't, gathered at the table to pray

To pray and to make it and to raise All-American children and
grandchildren taught to make it too.

Old men and women themselves, now, waiting at the
quarantine window to live or die.

What's the news.
When's the all clear sign.

There may not be an all clear sign, brother – just a temporary
end to the hostilities
And a list of the dead, hastily scrawled.

This one wrote a rock n roll anthem.
This one wrote checks to charities.
This one emptied bedpans at night.

This one filled the mouths of the poor.
This one was a priest in the Orthodox church.
This one lectured to empty rooms.
This one invested in slum buildings.
This one invested in stock futures.
This one ran thru money like a fish thru water.
This one drowned himself in a sea of movie scripts that he
sent to Hollywood and they sat on shelves for years and years
gathering dust.
This one owned a villa in Spain.
This one was a shrink in a cheap hotel.
This one ran a dance studio for troubled teens.

Bring out the dead, the hospital corridors are full of them.
The refrigerated truck is idling in the hospital parking lot.

Stack them up, ship them out
No time for flowers or funerals
No time for family goodbyes.
Just bury them now, or spread their ashes.
We'll remember them next Spring.
Under a yellow moon gone pink,
A yellow moon rising.

Mild Disturbance After Reading Kim Addonizio

At 5 pm one afternoon I said to myself
it's time to bake my potato

and couldn't think why it sounded dirty.
I had been reading Kim Addonizio

and wanted to talk to her about orgasms
how it doesn't matter

once you're past eighty
unless you have a young lover

which I don't, and don't want
anymore.

I had a friend
whose lover was younger than her kids.

He would eat their bananas
and forget to replace them.

It's the same with the old ones,
who forget.

Living alone, baking potatoes,
setting the table for one,

I bless this harsh freedom, no one
to pass me the sour cream.

Pass me the sour cream, I say to myself.

The End of Timing

"What time we waste, wasting time." – Charles Wright

Watching the numbers fall and rise.
Cursing the fools. Counting the dying.

Seasons hardly change where I live. Wind has its way.
I walk where it tells me.

I sing a *niggun* made of syllables and hunger, a song
I sang to my infant child before she had words.

It is a song of ancient tradition I made up for this time.

I cannot reach my child by plane, I cannot reach her children.
Who of us will be reached in time?

Who will watch reruns, bring wine and butter lettuce
to their elderly neighbors? Some will write wills.

Some will remember to practice their Czerny exercises,
unmask at last in front of an open window.

The Medium is the Messenger

My friend, who is a psychiatrist, scoffs
when I tell him I saw two clouds,
one dark, bristling with intimidation,
and next to it a fluffy white one, and
as I'm watching, the white cloud closes
over the dark one and gobbles it up.

Shouldn't it be seven white and seven dark,
he teases, referencing Pharaoh's dream,
the one that made Joseph prince of Egypt?
I get a scoff when I expect an inquisitive
eyebrow lift; he knows I'm not a prophet,
but hey, humor me for a minute.

Freudian that he is, fat cigars and pearly
clouds may just be facts, and nature
just nature banging up against nature –
pure coincidence – while I see the gods
flagging me. *Look up, I am sending you*
bouquets of white chrysanthemums.

The Border of What?

The train stops in the night
screeching, shuddering,
doors clattering,
uniformed men rushing through
dogs barking.
Where are we?
"At the *border*," mama whispers

Then she's gone with the uniforms.
I stare into the dark
where flashlights dance like drunken orbs
The *border* of what?

Why so many angry dogs?
Our luggage is still here, above the seats.

That counts, I think.
Right?

So I wait in the cold.
I will not cry!

The other day
dancing flashlights were all I had
to break the deep dark,
and dogs were again barking.
The picture of our luggage
flashed at the border of my mind
as I shivered under covers.
It's just a snowstorm, little one!
I told the frightened little girl,
as we waited in the frigid dark.
I will not cry!

Time Warp

The day is a gray vase with yellow flowers.
You can hear sparrows singing love songs,
watch the swarm of mayflies above the grass.

No cars on the road, no planes in the sky.
People walk six feet apart,
relish the movement of families, dogs, life.

We try to do it right:
hands raw from washing,
sewing machine busy with face masks,
sheltering in place as much as possible,
still feeling like when we were kids in the 1950s,
hiding from the atom bomb
under our desks.

Adrift

Our cellar still has the dark pocket
where one previous family stashed
rutabagas, potatoes, turnips, squash,
the shelves sticky with unwiped jars
of tomatoes and strawberries,
in case of a hard winter.

Now we wonder if we'll have enough
to get us through the unpredictable months,
possible shortages staring us down
like a scary stranger at the back door.

Wary of the new language, landscape, culture,
that are rising up to meet us,
we feel like immigrants,
standing on the deck of all we know,
the past around us in useless bundles.

Pandemic Fall

Blasting heat gives way
to sweet rains. At last, we draw
a collective breath.

A pink petunia,
awakened in gratitude
for her new pot, smiles.

At the lake, Spanish
voices ripple on the wind,
glide over rough stones.

New angles of light
dapple grass, reveal fall blooms.
Soft breezes heal me.

Priorities During a Pandemic at the Laundromat During the Soaps

The sky was a vapid teenager's eye-roll.
Birds were nattering.
A confusion of rain finally decided to pass.

Customers gathered like pilgrims waiting to land.
Clothes in the dryer rounded the turn like race horses.

A soap opera was on.
One of the characters had an incurable disease
easily transmitted to other minor actors
working on scale.

A news flash crawled over a television actor's forehead:
the pandemic reached new unheard-of heights.

Big deal, said the owner, angry her soaps were interrupted.
Now she won't know if the dying female was pregnant
from the married preacher who absconded money
from the collection plates.

The sky shifted its impatient feet.

Skin-Touch

Mingling has gone the way of horse and buggy.

Once, we could complain together at a store
about the rising cost of fruit,
or how schools have gone downhill
since we were kids.

We miss sitting in bleachers
during a snowstorm watching blowout football.
We want to rub a lamp to go back to the past.
Patience is virtuous, and too many lack virtue.

We see others acting crazed, not wearing masks.
They get up in our face, challenging us to do the same,
then we read about them dropping off like flies,
more springing up to spread the pandemic.
We can almost touch their lack of concern.

Lemmings are not the only ones herding over a cliff,
their leader pointing the way.

Winter Hair

I hear the songbirds more these days.
Try to decipher sirens & calls.

Tom makes a cocktail for us called black lily.
I grow out my white roots, winter hair.

Our calico wails at 3 am.
My mother's losing her hearing.

Figs fall from nearby trees.
Wild bobcat roams yards of shuttered homes.

I read somewhere that blue jays molt.
Unkempt they fly away.

George Floyd's Bench

On the metal bench outside the bar,
the place he used to sit in the afternoon sunshine,
a bouquet of balloons has appeared, jars of flowers,
a lit candle that quivers vigil in today's wind.
It's new since this morning, and now
I stop and breathe in this small quiet place.

A bicycle ticks and slows beside me,
the rider coming to cook what little is left
for curbside take-out in a mostly closed world.
These days, we all wear masks,
but our eyes meet. He says,
He worked here, you know,
and I tell him I know, point at my address next door.

These days we're not allowed
to reach out and hold each other.
We stand together for a while on the same street,
and there are no words.
I think we might be praying.
The balloons flicker and bounce against the brick,
against the sign that wishes him justice.
Finally, head bowed, he simply says,
He was my friend.

Plywood Shrines

I've walked the block to the grocery store
through last week's shrines of plywood.
It's odd to be indoors in boarded buildings.
All the lights are on, and there's a fluorescent
edge to the shelves, the check-out lines
where we stand on designated dots,
wearing masks, like extras in a scary movie.
News of an open store has traveled,
and it's quietly crowded.

On my block, there are spray-painted
prayers for justice, prayers for peace,
a mural surrounded by hearts.
Other sentiments have been sprayed over,
edited and layered.

Someday,
the plywood will come down
in a whine of power screwdrivers,
as suddenly as it appeared.
Even those small and precious scraps,
enough to stop a Molotov cocktail,
will vanish.

Someday the windows will be back,
and I wonder what we'll do
with everything we've prayed on plywood.

We live now

We live now by the side of the road. We live now inside with only small windows. We live now in the now. We live now in the hand in front of our faces. We live now where there is only a green screen we will fill in later. We live now in the why and not the because. We live now hoping the outside cars screeching by in the night will finally stop and let us sleep. We live now in the now. Not the now of five sentences ago. We live now in the now we couldn't imagine. We live now how we scream our names into the stale air of our apartments. We live now where we crack open the small windows, scream our names into the wind. We live now in remember and forget. In embrace and let go. We live now in the now.

Simple Enough

If you look at the moon a certain way it's a light bulb in the universe dark. It shines on the trees and the farms and the chickens clucking and pecking and the men walking their other women home before they go back to their wives. It lights up the haze that's been hanging for days like a garlic mist. It lights up the sculptures of coastlines, the Mediterranean lapping at the island shore. It shines on the breast of a woman whose heart is beating, keeps beating even after love has struck her down. It shines and shines and you wonder where the light switch is. Maybe behind some monster galaxy grate that scrapes the sky and you know one day that it will burn out anyway and no one will be tall enough to reach it, or in the mood enough to try and it'll just stay burnt out and broken, even though like anything else, it should be simple enough to change.

A Day in the Time of COVID

I am making fish soup. I am doing this without
a recipe; I hold the fish in my hands, lay it flat
on the cutting board, remove the head and tail,
scale the body of its scales, cut the belly down
the middle, and scrape out the guts. I put consommé
in a cast-iron pot and bring it to a simmer. I debone
the fish I caught during this pandemic, a freshwater
bottom feeder. If I then add carrots to the stock,
if I add scallions and kosher sea salt and garlic
and add a sprig of thyme and saffron threads,
if I say grace alone and consume my fare alone,
this is how I make peace with loss and how I pray.
I will save and freeze the leftovers; I will write
the details on an index card, because it's never easy,
never simple to be
prepared.

About the Poets

Calvin Ahlgren: During the pandemic, Calvin Ahlgren has kept on writing and reading poetry, gardening, teaching tai chi and qigong (by videoconference), walking his dogs and cooking, while the ascendancy of the virus and political grotesqueries changed so much around and within him and his loved ones. He tries to keep the faith and scratches his grateful.

Ellery Akers is the author of three books of poems, most recently, *Swerve: Environmentalism, Feminism, and Resistance.* She's won thirteen writing awards, including The Poetry International Prize, and her work has been featured in *The New York Times Magazine*, *Poetry*, and *American Life in Poetry*. She spends as much time as she can sitting in a camp chair on a wilderness trail, writing, drawing, and looking at birds.

Elaine Alarcon has been published in *Askew*, *Spillway*, *Solo*, *The Topanga Messenger*, and the *Denver Quarterly*. She loves zooming.

Malaika King Albrecht is the inaugural Heart of Pamlico Poet Laureate. She's the author of four poetry books – most recently, *The Stumble Fields*. She's founding editor of *Redheaded Stepchild*, an ezine that only accepts poems rejected elsewhere. She lives in Ayden, North Carolina on Freckles Farm with her family and is a yoga instructor, Reiki practitioner, and equine specialist in mental health and learning.

Kate Aver Avraham began her love relationship with words as a toddler, re-writing all her picture books! She co-edited *Second Wind: Words and Art of Hope and Resilience*, an anthology for her local Covid-19 Relief Fund. Blue Light Press published her chapbook, *Arms of My Longing*, in 2021. She is also a children's author, a former children's librarian, storyteller, singer/musician, and proud grandmother of four girls. A native of Santa Cruz, she now lives amidst the redwoods in Aptos, CA. Her pandemic sheltering has included writing, singing, lots of nature walks, and reaching out to others.

Lynn Axelrod is a community organizer along the Northern California coast. She's been a reporter for a weekly newspaper, an environmental

NGO staffer, a jewelry-maker, and an (early-retired) attorney. Her undergraduate and graduate studies were in Literature. In 2020 she spent her non-working hours grateful for her community's activist and arts bubble and Prartho Sereno's poetry group.

Kitty Baker: "Prose writer and long-time student of Prartho Sereno's Poetic Pilgrimage, where I've learned appreciation for poetry's economy of words to celebrate our shared humanity. As a young adult novelist, I care about impressions and values our young people take into the future. This strange period of isolation – a reset for all our daily habits and consumption – keys me to the beauty of this planet and the need to protect it. I spend my days hoping we will come out of this pandemic changed and wiser, with new habits that nurture and conserve every precious morsel of what nature so freely shares."

KB Ballentine's sixth book of poems, *The Light Tears Loose*, was published in 2019 by Blue Light Press. Her seventh, just published collection is *Edge of the Echo*. She spent the beginning of quarantine learning how to use Zoom to teach classes, then spent the summer reading, writing, and upgrading her technology skills. It was long overdue! She lives with her husband on Signal Mountain, Tennessee.

Anna Barnett shelters in Point Richmond, California, teaching Kindergarten in Mill Valley. When not in school, she spent most of 2020 cooking, reading, doing Zoom yoga, and hiking on the weekends. She is a student in Prartho Sereno's Poetic Pilgrimage class, where she plumbs and grapples with the realities and fantasies of the wild and shifting landscapes of America and the World.

Patricia Barone spends much of her time observing her prairie backyard and recently published *The Music of this Ruin* (Taj Mahal Press/ Cyberwit). She has also published *Your Funny, Funny Face* (Blue Light Press), *The Scent of Water* (Blue Light Press), *Handmade Paper* (New Rivers Press), and a novella, *The Wind*. She received a Loft-McKnight Award of Distinction in poetry, a Lake Superior Contemporary Writers Award for a short story, and a Minnesota State Arts Board Career Opportunity Grant for a workshop with Eavan Boland.

Beau Beausoleil is a poet and activist based in San Francisco. He is the author of fifteen books of poetry, including *A Glyphic House: New and Selected Poems 1976-2019*, published by Blue Light Press. The lockdown has caused him to study the interior of each ordinary day in a deep reflective manner. He addresses social justice issues with a clear understanding of the devastating effects of COVID-19 on the most vulnerable in our society.

Karen Benke writes for children and adults. She is author of a poetry chapbook, *Sister,* and four books of creative nonfiction. Her first in the series, *Rip the Page!* is translated into Russian, Korean, and Chinese. The mother of a college-aged son, during the Pandemic she has baked her way through a couple cookbooks, painted a few rooms, reorganized several bookshelves, applied for dual Italian citizenship for herself and eight family members, led dozens of writing adventures and, with dog Raz, hiked more trails than she can count.

Claudia Cole Bluhm: "Growing up on Liberty Street in San Francisco, my diary, Sarah, became my best friend. Life in the city filled her pages: fog racing over Twin Peaks each afternoon; my Gram, brother and I dipping jelly doughnuts into milked-down coffee on Saturday mornings; my brother and I ran around the neighborhood lost in adventures with the many kids on the block. Decades later, sheltering in place, San Francisco streets empty, the pandemic brought a halt to all our lives – particularly children's visits with Grams. I no longer tutor second and third graders in person, but found purpose working on the 2020 election – zooming and making calls, feeling a sense of strong community in such a solitary time. My debut book of poetry, *At the End of my Walk*, was published in 2021 by Blue Light Press."

Lita Marie Bonciolini is an artist and writer living in San Antonio, Texas. She spent her formative years in South Dakota, where the wide-open spaces fostered imagination, creativity, and a life-long curiosity about the world beyond. Lita's poetry was selected to accompany the Robert Indiana Art exhibit at the McNay Art Museum in San Antonio. The COVID-19 Pandemic, with its immeasurable impact on the world, has provided her with more time to explore her creativity, as well as spending time with family, friends, and her beloved dog, Leo.

Barbara Swift Brauer is the author of two books from Sixteen Rivers Press: *At Ease in the Borrowed World* and *Rain, Like a Thief.* She is a long-time member and former Board member of the Marin Poetry Center. "When the Shelter in Place restrictions first came in March, it seemed a writer's dream scenario: Staying home, no appointments, meetings, or lunch dates. Yet I immediately found it was all I could do to get through the day, let alone write. When I finally began writing, the poems were all about the pandemic. Thank goodness for birdsong and the solace of rural Marin that got me through those darkest early days."

Rosalind Brenner: "This home-bound, scared and trying-to-be-hopeful time has given me an opportunity to spend my days writing, painting and trying to finish a half-completed jigsaw puzzle while sitting in a daze on the window bench. Running a B&B in East Hampton has been so different than before. Super-vigilant, super-compliant, super-clean, always, but now...whew. My studio is my refuge. I feel grateful, but sad about the world." Her latest book of poems, *Every Glittering Chimera,* was published by Blue Light Press. She is also a painter and stained glass artist.

Judith Waller Carroll is the author of *What You Saw and Still Remember,* *The Consolation of Roses,* and *Walking in Early September.* Her poems have been read by Garrison Keillor on *The Writer's Almanac,* published in numerous journals and anthologies, and nominated for the Pushcart Prize and Best of the Net. Happiest when she is gardening, reading or writing poetry, she does not find staying home a hardship.

Mary Cavagnaro has been writing poetry since she was 11 years old. Reading and writing poetry are soul practices that bring her great joy. She lives with her partner under a benevolent redwood tree in Oakland. During this time of Covid, she is spending time coloring mandalas and walking the paths and streets of her neighborhood with her mask ready for the moments when she crosses path with others roaming the hilly streets.

Thomas Centolella is the author of four books of poetry, including *Almost Human,* winner of the Dorset Prize, selected by Edward Hirsch. Other honors include the Guggenheim Fellowship, the Lannan

Literary Award, and the California Book Award. He has taught creative writing in the Bay Area for many years, and lives at the top of one of San Francisco's major hills with his beloved Yamaha upright piano, which has been *instrumental* in his maintaining a modicum of sanity during a global pandemic. He has known the editor of this anthology since he was 20 years old but would never, ever hold that knowledge against her.

Kosrof Chantikian's book, *The Songs Inside of You*, was published June 2020 – his labor of love during the pandemic! He is also author of *Prophecies & Transformations* and *Imaginations & Self-Discoveries*. He is editor of *Octavio Paz: Homage to the Poet*, and *The Other Shore: 100 Poems by Rafael Alberti*; Editor of *KOSMOS: A Journal of Poetry*, and Series Editor of the Kosmos Modern Poets in Translations Series. "During the pandemic, I take long walks through the Corte Madera Marsh and Ring Mountain Open Space Reserve. The paths provide the beauty we need to see and touch. And sometimes we have lunch, discussions and laughter in our yard with friends (at a safe distance apart)."

Maxine Chernoff has published 6 books of fiction including a NYT-BR best collection of stories, *Signs of Devotion*, and 17 books of poetry. Her most recent is *Under the Music: Collected Prose Poems*, from Mad-Hat Press. Her poems and stories have appeared in numerous magazines and anthologies including *Conjunctions*, *The Paris Review*, *The Nation*, *The New Republic*, *The Iowa Review*, and *Journal of the Plague Year*. She is a winner of an NEA in poetry, and the PEN Translation Award, and she was a Visiting Writer at the American Academy in Rome. She is professor of Creative Writing at San Francisco State University and has also taught poetry at Naropa, the SLS in Russia, the Prague Summer Program for Writers, and Exeter University in England. She lives in Mill Valley.

Chris Cole is a multi-media artist living in the San Francisco Bay Area and also goes by the name, Disembodied Poetics. His novel, *Such Great Heights*, transplants *The Great Gatsby* to modern day Silicon Valley. He has a loyal internet following and publishes poetry and prose for both reputable and disreputable periodicals and anthologies. For the last decade he has helped run the San Francisco literary staple, Quiet Lightning.

Kat Crawford is a native San Franciscan and currently resides in Tiburon, California with her husband. She has been published in *Nomad's Choir, The Creative Woman, Marin Poetry Center Anthology, Spillway* and *Tuxedo*. Her book, *A Particular Heaven*, was published in 2014 and she has a new collection with Finishing Line Press. During Covid, her dogs, Lucy and Jagger, have provided daily entertainment sans masks! The IV drip of meditation, poetry classes with Prartho Sereno, and her Dominican University cohorts' cheerleading have all kept her in the middle of the lifeboat.

Lucille Lang Day is the award-winning author of seven full-length poetry collections, four poetry chapbooks, two children's books, and a memoir, *Married at Fourteen: A True Story*. In 2020, Blue Light Press published *Birds of San Pancho and Other Poems of Place*. She is the co-editor of two anthologies, *Fire and Rain: Ecopoetry of California* and *Red Indian Road West: Native American Poetry from California*. During the pandemic she has created five photo albums using some of the 6,900 photos on her iPhone and developed her cooking skills.

Marsha de la O's latest book, *Every Ravening Thing* (Pitt Poetry Series), came out in 2019. Her previous book, *Antidote for Night*, won the 2015 Isabella Gardner Award (BOA Editions). De La O is a founding member of the Ventura County Poetry Project, which produced *Dear America: Black Lives Matter*, a video of poems from writers of color responding to our current historical moment. She has spent her free time during the pandemic writing and gardening, and noticing like never before the courtship behavior of lizards. After the courtships, she waits for tiny lizard youth, no more than an inch or two in length. Even in October there were juveniles in the garden.

Michelle Demers holds an MFA from Vermont College of Fine Arts and has been published in numerous literary journals and anthologies. Her full-length poetry collection, *Green Mountain Zen*, was published in 2019 by Blue Light Press. Michelle Demers was fortunate to spend the COVID-19 lockdown with her amiable husband Michael and sweet cat Lucie in Williston, Vermont.

Diana Donovan: A graduate of Brown University, Diana Donovan is a freelance writer and marketing consultant based in Mill Valley, California. During the pandemic, she spent much of her newfound time going on long walks, cooking comfort foods, and finally upgrading to a premium Zoom subscription. When libraries opened up, she was also a frequent curbside pickup junkie.

Claudia Jensen Dudley taught for many years with California Poets in the Schools, bringing poetry and storytelling of myth cycles and folktales to San Francisco students. Also a pianist, she has set her own and student poetry to music in three song cycles. She's spent this quiet last year in walks to her community garden, work on an "impossible" piece of music, and gathering years of poems into a book, *Grace at Midwinter*.

Cyra Sweet Dumitru lives on a hilltop near San Antonio, Texas. From this vantage point she watched red-tail hawks, great horned owls, turkey buzzards, and white herons fly, glide, hunt, and perch, reminding her that natural cycles prevail during pandemic too. Frequent swims, going for walks, delighting in the antics of her young cats, writing and revising poems, learning to cook with eggplant, facilitating virtual Poetry Circles as a poetic medicine practitioner, and weekly outreach to nurses and hospital staff have been mainstays of her stay-at-home months.

Stephen Dunn's most recent book of poems, *Pagan Virtues*, was published by Norton. He won the Pulitzer Prize for *Different Hours* Among his many other awards, *Loosestrife* was a finalist for the Nation? Book Critics Circle award, and he's received Fellowships from tl Guggenheim and Rockefeller Foundations. Stephen tells us: "Duri the pandemic I've been home writing and reading, and occasion enjoying being a truly masked man."

Rebecca Ellis lives in southern Illinois along the Mississippi f She watches the waterfowl that move through the air and alo river, and credits the joy of spotting mergansers, loons, and g for getting her through the pandemic. Her poems can be f *About Place Journal, Bellevue Literary Review, The American J Poetry, Naugatuck River Review, Ekphrastic Review, Prairi* and *Crab Creek Review*.

Johanna Ely served as the sixth poet laureate of Benicia from 2016-2018. Her latest book of poetry, *Postcards From a Dream*, was published by Blue Light Press in 2020. During the first months of the pandemic, she read lots of poetry books and zoomed with her poetry group, watched too many shows on Netflix, and exercised to work-out videos on YouTube. She and her husband also fixed up their basement, turning it into a studio, a salon, and a gallery space. She hopes to host a poetry salon in her home when people are able to meet again.

Linda Enders, musician and art enthusiast, loves poetry and literature. She studies poetry with Prartho Sereno, attends writing retreats at Santa Sabina Center and writing workshops at Ghost Ranch in New Mexico. She lives with her artist husband, Bernd Enders, at the edge of open space in Terra Linda, California. The pandemic has been a puzzling time, but they've not done a single jigsaw puzzle. She writes every day. He paints. And they've learned many things: they don't mind being home together; it's possible to acquire most everything you need without leaving home; and finches, sparrows, quail, owls and coyotes are very good company.

Heather Saunders Estes is the author of *Inner Sunset* and *Cloudbreak*. She left her 37-year career as CEO of Planned Parenthood Northern California to write poetry, draw, garden, and advocate for homeless LGBTQIA+ youth. During COVID, Heather, her professor husband, and biologist daughter are all ferociously writing in their San Francisco home. They share laughs, friends, mutual editing, and pie.

Kathy Evans loves books, looking at them, reading them, finding places for them to live in her 1889 apartment complex, located by the library in San Rafael. She has four poetry books: *Imagination Comes To Breakfast* (child raising/marriage years), *Hunger and Sorrow* (winner of the Small Press Poetry Prize), *As the Heart Is Held* (post marriage years), and most recently *Trespassers Welcome* (Blue Light Press.) During the pandemic she has baked and cooked new recipes – corn chowder, a fabulous eggplant parmesan, and the old favorite – pumpkin cookies. To keep from sinking into the mire, she has planted, baked, painted the doors and the deck, and passed amusing time with her grandchildren, She has hiked the Mt. Tam trails with her son, who claims she is too slow!

Catlyn Fendler is a poet, nonfiction writer, teacher and consultant whose work has been published in a variety of journals and anthologies. She was editor of the *2016 Marin Poetry Center Anthology*, and holds an MFA from the Iowa Writers' Workshop. She has led workshops on creativity and spirituality and taught poetry writing as spiritual practice in the College of Marin Community Education program. She has spent much of her life roaming the wilds of the American West, although during the pandemic her wanderings have been confined to the redwoods of coastal California and the wonders of her of hometown, Larkspur.

Elsa Fernandez: "Give me some skin, baby!" he told her every morning. He loved the warmth when their hands touched. After torturous months in hospitals, Elsa and her partner were home and loving the solitude. Elsa was facing a double impact to her life and emotions – caring for her dying partner in the midst of a Pandemic. But as she recalls, "The Pandemic never felt so good! It gave us a gift like no other – time together to fill with joy and discovery." The Pandemic taught her precious lessons. Fight for life as long as you can, but don't be afraid to cross the river.

Stewart Florsheim has been widely published in magazines and anthologies, and has received several awards for his work. He was editor of *Ghosts of the Holocaust*, an anthology of poetry by children of Holocaust survivors. His books include *The Girl Eating Oysters, The Short Fall From Grace* (Blue Light Book Award), and *A Split Second of Light*, which received an Honorable Mention in the San Francisco Book Festival. Stewart spent his time during the pandemic trying to hide in his day job, occasionally looking for moments of inspiration.

Diane Frank is author of eight books of poems, two novels, and a photo memoir of her 400 mile trek in the Nepal Himalayas. *While Listening to the Enigma Variations: New and Selected Poems* was published in 2021 by Glass Lyre Press. Diane teaches at San Francisco State University and Dominican University, and plays cello in the Golden Gate Symphony. "We were rehearsing Mahler's First Symphony when our orchestra shut down. Now, I'm playing the Bach Unaccompanied Cello Suites at home and playing duets with Jill Brindel twice a month."

Joyce Futa has been writing poetry since she retired in 2001. Her book, *Lit Windows: A Book of Haibun and Tanka Prose*, was published in 2017 by Blue Light Press. She lives in Altadena, California, a small community where her life consists of many small routines – walking her dog, reading and writing, gardening, and until March of this year, hanging out with friends and family. Since the pandemic's arrival, the lack of social interactions has made big hole in her feelings of general contentment. To make up for this, she has taken up new activities – jigsaw puzzles, ceramics, macrame. It helps somewhat. Her house is a mess.

Jeannine Hall Gailey served as the second Poet Laureate of Redmond, Washington. She's the author of five books of poetry: *Becoming the Villainess, She Returns to the Floating World, Unexplained Fevers, The Robot Scientist's Daughter*, and *Field Guide to the End of the World*, winner of the Moon City Press Book Prize and the SFPA's Elgin Award. Her work has appeared in *American Poetry Review, Ploughshares*, and *Poetry*. She spent most of her quarantine bird-watching and photographing scenes around her neighborhood.

Lisha Adela García is a poet and small business advisor with the UTSA San Antonio Small Business Development Center. She works from both sides of her brain and seeks humor wherever she can. Her dogs are now very familiar with Zoom manners and protocols. She is author of two books – *Blood Rivers* and *A Rope of Luna*, both published by Blue Light Press. She was recently featured in the anthology, *Dreams and Blessings*, published by Blue Light Press.

Marilyn Gaynes practiced the art of psychotherapy for almost 50 years, taught modern dance in Santa Barbara and Scotland, convened process groups for activists, and currently studies poetry-making, Tibetan Buddhism and qi gong. She thought she'd learn Spanish during the pandemic, but so far, hasn't. She lives with her husband in Fairfax, California, and is a great-grandmother.

Melanie Gendron, book designer for Blue Light Press, is a painter, graphic artist, and poet. Her visionary art gained international attention with the publication of *The Gendron Tarot Book and Deck*.

Her publications include *This Fool's Journey: Through Tarot's 22 Major Arcana* (Blue Light Press); *Dreaming The Light, The Elemental Goddess*, and *Metatron: Angel of The Presence* (River Sanctuary Publishing). Her poetry appears in the *River of Earth and Sky: Poems for the Twenty-First Century* anthology (Blue Light Press). Before, and during being sheltered in place, she has run her graphic arts business, Gendron Studios, in the Santa Cruz Mountains of California.

Diane Glancy has been home since March 2020. She is professor emerita at Macalester College. Her latest book, *Island of the Innocent, a Consideration of the Book of Job*, was published by Turtle Point Press in 2020. In this unending year of 202020202020, she is grateful for words. She has been writing a play, *Decoy*, for Native Voices at the Autry, along with poems and essays.

Karen Pierce Gonzalez: Sheltering in place allows Karen to travel to new places in writing and art. These days, she zooms into poetic and fictional landscapes with fellow poets and is currently creating a series of cradle basket assemblages, using recycled and natural materials, cultural folklore, and prayers for patience. Her poems have appeared in *BluePepper, Postcard Poems & Prose*, and *Voice of Eve*.

Hiroko Goto is 100 years old this year. She lives in Oshino Village, Yamanashi, Japan. She was born into a high class samurai family in Tokyo and learned about Buddhism from her grandmother. After marriage, she and her one-year-old son escaped the bombings and found shelter in the countryside. Then she returned to a tough life in Tokyo. She has taught Japanese tea ceremony for 56 years, and has taught Japanese calligraphy since 1954. In 1967 she walked from Kyoto to Tokyo, praying each step of the way for peace for the souls on both sides lost during the war. After her pilgrimage, she became a lay priestess with the Jakoin temple in Kyoto.

Bill Graeser writes his poems out loud – even when wearing a mask, repeating what lines he has until the next line spills out. He is author of *Fire in a Nutshell*, has been published in the *North American Review* and on many a refrigerator – and is winner of the Iowa Poetry Association's 2012 Norman Thomas Memorial Award. Bill has worked as carpenter, dairy farmer and is currently the locksmith at Maharishi International University, Fairfield, Iowa.

Carol Griffin lives in Marin County. Along with writing poems, she explores expressive arts for healing and has a Sufi meditation practice. Love of nature, self-inquiry, and a passion for what it means to be human infuse her life and work. She is self-employed as a personal assistant, helping elders. Carol's poems are published in the *Marin Poetry Center Anthology, Birdland Journal, DoveTales Literary Journal,* and *California Quarterly.* During the Pandemic she has been on zoom retreats, made fig jam and is learning to be an antiracist.

John Harn grew up in Michigan and spent his adult life in Oregon. He is the author of *Physics for Beginners* (Blue Light Press) and *Witness* (Aldrich Press). His poems have appeared in *Denver Quarterly, Miramar, New Orleans Review, Pleiades, Prairie Schooner, Spillway* and other journals. He spent his quarantine time wading in the Gulf of Mexico and working on a new collection, *The Real and the Not So.* He is co-author of three daughters and co-editor of a rambunctious grandson.

Katherine Hastings is the author of three full-length collections of poetry, most recently *Shakespeare & Stein Walk Into a Bar.* She spent the first spring of the pandemic hiding from the world, the summer floating socially distanced on the Niagara River, the fall hiking in various parks, and the winter teaching an on-line poetry class that resulted in a chapbook published by the Small Change Series of WordTemple Press. A Northern California native, she moved with her partner to an island on the Niagara River between New York and Canada following the wildfires of 2017.

Margie Heckelman: "I had the privilege and fun of growing up in my father's youth circus in Washington State, every summer a wild ride of travels and performances at county fairs and football fields along the West Coast and several other states. My adult life has been filled with the love of family, travels, nature, and a desire to write poetry as my creative escape. The spring shutdown found me hard at work in the garden with my daughter, baking cookies and zucchini bread, and going on daily walks to keep all in perspective."

True Heitz: "I am a very important person. I have been taught the art of lying by the President of the United States: I have written 7 poetry books that have been translated into 47 languages and distributed to 70 countries. I have taught Child Growth and Development at the college level and was a K-6 Open Classroom School Teacher for 30 years. During the Pandemic, I made a huge life transition, moving from my home in Fairfax, California to the Redwoods Senior Community in Mill Valley. I started with 14 days of quarantine alone in my room, writing poetry, and learning to love masks. My puppy, Poppy, likes our new home."

Jane Hirshfield's ninth collection of poetry, *Ledger* (Knopf), came out March 10, 2020, the day everything changed in the U.S. She spent the first months of sheltering-in-place learning how to give Zoom readings and workshops; record videos, radio, and podcasts; and completing interviews and exchanges with other poets (including Mark Doty, Kaveh Akbar, Ellery Akers, and Ilya Kaminsky). A former chancellor of the Academy of American Poets, Hirshfield's poems appear in *The New Yorker*, *The Atlantic*, *The New York Review of Books*, *The New York Times*, *Poetry*, and ten editions of *The Best American Poetry*. In 2019, she was inducted into the American Academy of Arts & Sciences.

Jodi Hottel's most recent chapbook is *Out of the Ashes* from Pandemonium Press. Her previous chapbooks are *Voyeur* (WordTech Press, 2017) and *Heart Mountain*, winner of the 2012 Blue Light Press Poetry Prize. Jodi is currently sheltering-in-place in Santa Rosa, California, where she has taken up the jigsaw puzzle craze.

Erik Ievins: Music has always been a comfortable second language for Erik Ievins. Classically trained on cello since he was old enough to hold a bow, Erik joined professional symphony and pops orchestras while still in high school. He plays for contra dances, Scottish dances, and English Country dances with StringFire, and volunteers in the cello section of the Golden Gate Symphony. When collaborating with poets, he expresses the emotions of the poem through music. From time to time, when he is not tinkering with cars or rebuilding houses, he is moved to document his surroundings with the written word.

Donna Isaac is a teaching artist who organizes community readings and workshops through the League of Minnesota Poets. Her books includes *Footfalls* (Pocahontas Press); *Tommy* (Red Dragonfly Press); *Holy Comforter* (Red Bird Chapbooks); and *Persistence of Vision* (Finishing Line Press). During the pandemic lock-down, she has been tending a small garden, taking walks, revising poems, and cooking like a madwoman, trying out new and eclectic recipes like red beans and rice and Greek stuffed vegetables. After the pandemic, she hopes to travel, continue writing, offer community classes, and see more of her family.

Susie James lives in rural Iowa. Her poetry has been published in journals and magazines including *The MacGuffin, Lyrical Iowa, Sierra Magazine* and in several anthologies. Her first book of poems, *Under a Prairie Moon* was published in 2007 by Blue Light Press. She has spent the last pandemic year walking in nature, gardening and writing.

Lois P. Jones' first collection, *Night Ladder,* was published in 2017 by Glass Lyre Press. Awards include the Lascaux Poetry Prize, the Bristol Poetry Prize, and the Tiferet Poetry Prize. Lois has work published in *Plume, Guernica Editions, New Voices: Contemporary Writers Confronting the Holocaust; Verse Daily* and *Tupelo Quarterly.*

Ami Kaye's poems, reviews, and articles have appeared in various publications including *Kyoto Journal, Comstock Review, Naugatuck River Review,* and *Diode.* Her writing received nominations for the Pushcart and James B. Baker Prizes. Ami is the publisher & editor at Glass Lyre Press. Her new book, *Flutesongs of Tanjore,* will be published by Salmon Poetry in 2022.

Helga Kidder lives in the Tennessee hills with her husband, a multitude of woodland birds, and birdseed-stealing squirrels. She wiles her time writing poetry in the aroma of a scent-spewing apparatus and a two-wicked candle until the muse begs for rest. She has four collections of poetry, *Wild Plums, Luckier than the Stars, Blackberry Winter,* and *Loving the Dead,* which won the 2020 Blue Light Book Award.

Anna Kodama paints and writes in eastern Pennsylvania, a few miles from the Delaware River. 2020 was meant to be the year she spent in New York City, getting to know the museums and babysitting the grandchild who would be born in May. The Corona Trickster had a different idea! Matilda True was born on April 24 in Pennsylvania, and for the first half of her life, instead of stroller rides in Astoria Park or subway trips to the MOMA, she was carried through the woods and rocked on the green porch swing

Ted Kooser is a poet and essayist, a Presidential Professor of English at the University of Nebraska-Lincoln. He served as the U. S. Poet Laureate from 2004-2006, and his book *Delights & Shadows* won the 2005 Pulitzer Prize for poetry. His writing is known for its clarity, precision and accessibility. He worked for many years in the life insurance business, retiring in 1999 as a vice president. He and his wife, Kathleen Rutledge, the retired editor of *The Lincoln Journal Star*, live near the village of Garland, Nebraska.

Jacqueline Kudler lives in Sausalito, California and teaches classes in memoir writing and literature at the College of Marin. She is author of two books, *Sacred Precinct*, (Sixteen Rivers Press) and *Easing into Dark*. She was awarded the Marin Arts Council Board Award for outstanding work in 2005, and the Marin Poetry Center Lifetime Achievement Award in 2010. She feels that holding on to some semblance of sanity in these times is nothing short of miraculous, by maintaining loving human contact through Zoom and long walks with dear friends – masked and socially distanced, of course.

Laurie Kuntz's new poetry collection, *The Moon Over My Mother's House*, is forthcoming from Finishing Line Press. Her chapbook, *Women at the Onsen* was published by Blue Light Press, and *Simple Gestures* won the Texas Review Press Chapbook Contest. Her poetry has been nominated for a Pushcart Prize and Best of the Net. During the pandemic, she avoided organizing her underwear drawer and focused more on filling every vase in her house with something in bloom.

Melody Lacina, a native Iowan, now lives in Berkeley, California. Her book, *Private Hunger*, was published as part of the University of Akron Press poetry series. Another manuscript or two are in the tinkering stage. During the shelter in place, she and her husband dodged each other as they worked from home. Long walks and swimming (once their pool reopened) kept them sane.

Jennifer Lagier is a retired educator who lives near the Pacific Ocean with two rescue dogs, half a block from the stage where Jimi Hendrix torched his guitar. Her work appears in *From Everywhere a Little: A Migration Anthology, Fire and Rain: Ecopoetry of California, Missing Persons: Reflections on Dementia, Silent Screams: Poetic Journeys Through Addiction & Recovery.* Her newest books are *Dystopia Playlist* (Cyber-Wit) and *Meditations on Seascape and Cypress* (Blue Light Press).

Rustin Larson's poetry has appeared in *The New Yorker, The Iowa Review,* and *North American Review.* He won 1st Editor's Prize from *Rhino* and was a prize winner in The National Poet Hunt and The Chester H. Jones Foundation contests. A graduate of the Vermont College MFA in Writing, Larson was an Iowa Poet at The Des Moines National Poetry Festival, and a featured poet at the Poetry at Round Top Festival. During the pandemic Rustin has produced watercolor paintings and has taught his cat Finnegan karate.

Dorianne Laux: "Life hasn't changed much for me during the pandemic. I read, I write, I binge watch. I've been gardening, cleaning out old files, closets, drawers, and tossing what I no longer need. I've been doing what I always do when I have time on my hands, puzzles. It reminds me that the broken can be reassembled, which is what we are in the process of doing right now as a people, as a country."

Carey Link is a retired civil servant from Huntsville, Alabama and is nearing the completion of her M.S. in counseling from Faulkner University. She hopes to one day counsel clients living with life-altering illness. Her chapbooks include *To Light a House of Bones* (Blue Light Press), *Through the Kaleidoscope* (Blue Light Press), *What it Means to Climb a Tree,* and *I Walk a Frayed Tightrope Without a Safety Net* (Finishing Line Press). Since 2018, Carey has been a poetry writing mentor for The Handy, Uncapped Pen online program. During the pandemic Carey has had time write and grow as a poet.

Jeremy Littman: Born in San Francisco, grew up in Marin – degrees in English Literature and Architecture. Deeply blessed with an extraordinary wife, three wonderful children, a daughter-in-law and one glorious granddaughter. Work was building and renovating fine buildings in San Francisco, part of the fabric of the city. My passions are family, playing in the wild, reading, painting and now poetry. I will never know what happens in a single afternoon except this seat in the sun, this next breath, this garden to tend.

Ellaraine Lockie is a successful and highly awarded poet, nonfiction author and essayist . . . at least she was until the Coronavirus infected her Muse. Blue Light Press became her personal vaccine with its calls for submissions that have jolted her from months of closet/drawer cleaning, obsessive TV series, baking/eating (too much) bread and long hours of making one sheet of handmade paper after another in her papermaking studio. Thank you, Blue Light Press.

Naomi Ruth Lowinsky finds solace and release in writing poetry during the pandemic. Hibernation comes naturally to her, and she is grateful for more slow time in her life to pay attention to her dreams and let them nurture her poems. And yet, she is haunted by the horrors of our times, the unnecessary dead, the cruelty. Poems are her way to protest, her way to envision a better world. Her fifth collection of poems, *Death and His Lorca*, was published by Blue Light Press in 2021. Lowinsky is winner of the Blue Light Poetry Prize and the Obama Millennial Award. She is a Jungian Analyst, a member of the San Francisco Jung Institute, and Poetry Editor for *Psychological Perspectives.*

Terry Lucas is Poet Laureate Emeritus of Marin County, California. He has spent much of his shelter-in-place time in Las Cruces, New Mexico, researching the archives in preparation for editing an anthology of essays and interviews about his first poetry professor, Keith Wilson. During several 19-hour drives, he has listened to almost the entire discography of Steely Dan. Terry's latest book is *The Thing Itself* (Longship Press, 2020) with photographs by Gary Topper. More about Terry and his work as a poetry coach can be found at www.terrylucas.com.

Jeanne Lupton has been on retreat at home since March 17, 2020, lost 25 pounds on purpose, had a spiritual reawakening, has written poems, turned 75 years old, told her life story in ten minutes, said good-bye to her beloved cat Summer, and walked one mile most days. The best year of her life so far. She hosted Frank Bette Center for the Arts Second Saturdays Poetry and Prose Reading Series for 13 years. Her new book, *Love is a Tanka*, was just published by Blue Light Press.

Emilie Lygren is a poet and outdoor science educator who loves talking to strangers, taking long walks, cooking for friends, and reading. Emilie has developed dozens of publications and curricula focused on outdoor science education and social-emotional learning through her work at the award-winning BEETLES Project at the Lawrence Hall of Science. Her first book of poetry, *What We Were Born For*, was published by Blue Light Press in 2021.

Matthew MacLeod lives in northern Ontario, Canada. During the pandemic he returned to writing poetry, playing classical guitar, listening to the radio, and began walking a dog for an octogenarian neighbor. Back when Pluto used to be a planet, Matthew was the editor of the *The Dryland Fish – An Anthology of Contemporary Iowa Poetry*. His first full length book of poetry, *St. Distraction*, is forthcoming.

Ed Meek's fourth book of poems, *High Tide*, has just come out. He has been spending a lot of time during the pandemic reading, writing and taking naps. Afternoons, he walks his labradoodle, Mookie, whom he will never trade, no matter what the offer.

Nancy Lee Melmon lives in Sedona, Arizona, a land where the red rocks still kneel down at night and pray for rain. She loves words, so she writes poetry. She is coauthor of *Dreams and Blessings, Six Visionary Poets*, published by Blue Light Press. During the pandemic she created a sanctuary for the birds outside her office patio – with suet hangers, feeders, and a special bird bath decorated with spiraling Suns and Kokopellis. For Nancy Lee, poems, like birds, are alive. Each one has a heart, wings, and their own song. Poems remind us, like Kokopelli and the birds, that we too are storytellers, teachers, healers, and that we too have the ability to sing a beautiful future into existence.

Megan Merchant has been smudging paint, splicing collages, and learning how to play the didgeridoo while confined to her home for the past year. She is also the author of four full-length collections.

The latest, *Before the Fevered Snow*, was released at the start of the pandemic with Stillhouse Press. Her most recent awards include a drawing of a mermaid from her son for being the World's Best Mom and the Inaugural Michelle Boisseau Prize with Bear Review. She is an Editor at *Pirene's Fountain* and *The Comstock Review*.

Phyllis Meshulam is the Poet Laureate of Sonoma County, having received this honor just as the pandemic broke out. So much for those carefully thought-out projects! So, instead of providing in-services for classroom teachers, she's created videos of reliable lessons to help spread the good news of poetry to children in Sonoma County. She has taught with California Poets in the Schools since 1999, serving as Sonoma County area coordinator for nine years, and as coordinator for the county's Poetry Out Loud program for thirteen years. She was editor for *Poetry Crossing*, a lesson plan book for CalPoets' 50th anniversary. She has five collections of poems, most recently *Land of My Father's War*.

Angie Minkin has lived in San Francisco for 40 years and is grateful to live in this cool, gray city filled with sea light. She raised two children in San Francisco's Excelsior District and now shares her home with her husband and two playful cats. Yoga, dance, and poetry have kept her focused during the pandemic. Angie is inspired by the political landscape, poetry of liberation, and the voice of the wise woman. She is proud to be a coauthor of the recently published *Dreams and Blessings, Six Visionary Poets* (Blue Light Press). A poetry editor with *Vistas & Byways*, her work has appeared in that journal and several others.

Hallie Moore is a West Coast poet who has found herself living in Texas for the last 30 plus years. A retired English instructor, she has become enmeshed in the jigsaw puzzle exchange community and now knows more about the minutiae of Birds of North America, Herbs and Wildflowers, foreign words for umbrellas, and Charles Winsocki's Americana than any non-pandemic shut-in would ever care to know.

MJ Moore lives in the San Francisco Bay Area. Her various incarnations have included technical writer, environmental activist, farm apprentice, teacher, poet, Buddhist practitioner, wife and mother.

Her odd collection of skills includes milking goats, driving a tractor, editing books on meditation and library format integration, directing first-grade plays, and chanting mantras in Pali. During the pandemic, her first book of poems, *Topography of Dreams*, was published by Blue Light Press, and she embraced interpretive Qi Gong, to the puzzlement of her neighbors.

Claudine Nash is a psychologist and award-winning author of five poetry books. She writes extensively about loss, healing and the liberation of releasing the past. Winner of the 2020 Blue Light Book Award for *Beginner's Guide to Loss in the Multiverse*, her poetry can be found in a wide-range of publications including *Asimov's Science Fiction*, *BlazeVOX*, and *Cloudbank*. Claudine is an essential worker in New York and spent the darkest days of the Spring of 2020 providing emotional and psychological support to the frontline medical workers at the hard-hit inner-city hospital where she works.

Annie Klier Newcomer resides in Prairie Village, Kansas. She is a member of the *Key West Cigar Factory Poets' Group*. She provides poetry and playwriting classes at Turning Point, a Center for Hope and Healing through the University of Kansas Medical Center for patrons with chronic illnesses. She is a contributing writer for *FlapperPress* and her poetry has been published in Great Britain, Australia, New Zealand and the Midwest.

Stephanie Noble teaches a weekly women's meditation class on Zoom and is the author of *Asking In, Six Empowering Questions Only You Can Answer*. Her dharma talks can be found at Stephanienoble.com. Her poems have been published in numerous journals and anthologies.

Barbara Novack is Writer-in-Residence and member of the English Department at Molloy College. In normal times she hosts the Poetry Events reading series on campus, and conducts creative writing workshops in the community. During the shutdown in the spring, her safe space was sitting at her kitchen window, where she looked out at her backyard, writing poems about blossoms, birds, and the world according to COVID-19.

Naomi Shihab Nye is the Young People's Poet Laureate (Poetry Foundation). She has spent much lockdown time gardening and reading books with her 4-year-old grandson, Connor James, who regularly says, "We're BOTH poets." Her most recent book is *Everything Comes Next: New and Selected Poems* (Greenwillow, 2020).

Eugene O'Connor is a poet living with his husband in Columbus, Ohio. "I write," he says, "to ward off grief during this pandemic, which has taken so many lives." Given the isolation necessitated by social distancing, Eugene has begun a series of poems in which he imagines himself a traveler suddenly stranded on a remote island. To make up for his exile, Eugene's persona works on developing shamanistic abilities. He finds poetry "an incredible source of solace during these dark and turbulent times. I look to my favorite poets, old and new, to recover those truths that only poetry can tell us."

Nynke Salverda Passi was born and raised in the Netherlands. She's been published in *Calyx, Gulf Coast, Poetry Breakfast, Red River Review*, and the anthologies *River of Earth and Sky* and *Carrying the Branch*. She is a teacher and mentor to young poets and writers. Her favorite place to write is with a cat on her lap and a view of Louden Pond, where Canada geese pass twice every year to share their gossip and stories.

Marge Piercy is the author of 20 poetry collections, most recently *Made in Detroit* (Knopf); and *On the Way Out Turn Off the Light*, (Knopf, 2020). She has also published 17 novels, most recently *Sex Wars*; a short story collection; *The Cost of Lunch, Etc.*, a memoir; *Sleeping with Cats*; and four non-fiction books. "During Covid I have written as usual, have done clunky Zoom readings, gardened and lately, I see friends – outside and at a distance."

Ken Pobo is author of *Bend of Quiet*, winner of the 2014 Blue Light Poetry Prize. "During the pandemic, I retired. My last eight weeks of teaching were on Zoom. This was exhausting. Summer came and there wasn't much to do except be in the garden. That was a pleasure except for a period of rainlessness and critters who dared to chomp on seedlings and tender shoots. Mostly I read, write, and in good weather sit on the porch with my husband and the cats. I'm surprised that I haven't watched more films. With winter coming, that may change."

Barbara Quick's fourth novel, *What Disappears*, set in the world of the Ballets Russes, will be published by Regal House in May 2022. Her debut poetry chapbook, *The Light on Sifnos*, was winner of the 2020 Blue Light Press Poetry Prize. She had five poems recorded by Garrison Keillor and featured on The Writer's Almanac in 2021. Based on a small farm and vineyard in the California Wine Country, Barbara loves organic gardening and Brazilian dancing with equal fervor.

Jane Rades is from Wisconsin and has lived in San Francisco since 1963. She has two books of poetry, *Five Decades, A Rosary of Poems* and *Midnight at Mom and Dad's*. She has also published *Two Years in the Tarot, Portrait of the Artist as a Young Fortuneteller* and a Tarot deck, *The 1969 Tarot*. Since the lock-down, she started scanning photos from all of the trips she took in the 1990's and early 2000's, with an eye to putting them online to create travelogues. It has given her a great focus in these times of not being able to socialize as much as before.

Stuart P. Radowitz just had his first collection, a ten-year compilation, *Snow Hangs on the Branches of Evergreens*, published by Blue Light Press. He has spent most of the last ten months realizing being a recluse is not always fun.

Deborah Ramos, a San Diego poet with mermaid hair, is the author of *from the earthen drum of my body*. She performed before a live audience in Dublin, Ireland in February 2020, right before the world shut down. Pre-pandemic, Deborah hosted readings at the Poetry Bench in Balboa Park. Sheltering in place, days found her watching re-runs of the Wendy Williams show and stress eating with her cats, while quiet nights found her binge watching on Netflix and sampling various Irish whiskeys.

Claudia M. Reder is the author of *How to Disappear* (Blue Light Press); *Uncertain Earth* (Finishing Line Press), and *My Father & Miro* (Bright Hill Press). *How to Disappear* was awarded first prize in the Pinnacle and Feathered Quill awards. She also won the Charlotte Newberger Poetry Prize from *Lilith Magazine*. She is recently retired from teaching at California State University at Channel Islands. She has also been a poet/storyteller in the Schools. During the pandemic, she has become even more hermetic. While she worries about the world, she stays home and zooms with poets and students, and writes, and writes.

Susan Rogers is a practitioner of Sukyo Mahikari – a spiritual practice promoting positivity. During this time of pandemic, protest and the wearing of masks, she has tried to encourage others by smiling with her eyes. She has found peace and comfort walking among the trees in her neighborhood, marveling at the beauty of their branches against the sky. Her poetry has been published in *Altadena Poetry Review, California Quarterly, Carrying the Branch: Poets in Search of Peace, Kyoto Journal, Pirene's Fountain, San Diego Poetry Annual: The Best Poems of San Diego*, and *Tiferet*.

Alice Elizabeth Rogoff, as an Editor of the *Haight Ashbury Literary Journal*, still receives manuscripts by mail, many from prisoners. During social distancing, she writes songs and is growing a very large pumpkin. She won the Blue Light Book Award for her poetry book *Mural*. Her most recent book, *Painting the Cat's Vision*, was also published by Blue Light Press.

Trudy Roughgarden has lived in the San Francisco Bay Area since 1972. She teaches piano and is very active in the music, Scottish, English and ballroom dance communities. During the Covid shelter in place, she has alternated her time between the industrious creativity possible with isolation (creating music and dances) and the existential paralysis of isolation (missing friends dearly).

Janice D. Rubin is a counselor and educator. Her work has appeared in *Timberline Review, CIRQUE*, and *Red River Review* among others. In 2019 her book, *Tin Coyote*, was nominated for the Stafford/Hall Award for Poetry. She's the author of *Transcending Damnation Creek Trail & Other Poems* (Flutter Press) and *Tin Coyote* (Blue Light Press). During the pandemic and enforced writing retreat, she's been diligently working on her third book of poems.

Mary Kay Rummel's ninth poetry book, *Nocturnes: Between Flesh and Stone* was published by Blue Light Press in 2020. *The Lifeline Trembles*, won the 2014 Blue Light Book Award. A former poet laureate for Ventura County, CA, she co-edited *Psalms of Cinder & Silt*, poems by survivors of California wildfires for Solo Press. Dividing her time between Minneapolis and Ventura, she has spent hours on the highways seeing firsthand the differences in how people are behaving during this pandemic. She is grateful for the poetry and the poets who have been her inspiration and source of community these past months.

Marjorie Saiser's *The Track the Whales Make: New & Selected Poems* will be published in 2021 in Ted Kooser's series at University of Nebraska Press. *Losing the Ring in the River* (University of New Mexico Press) won the Willa Award. Her work has been published in *Prairie Schooner, Alaska Quarterly, Poetry East, Rattle, Chattahoochee, Briar Cliff,* and *Nimrod.* During the pandemic, her respite became the *L.A. Times* Crossword, a cup of coffee, and a window looking out into the trees.

Barbara Saxton engages in a weird, wide range of interests and activities: performing classical, folk and Eastern European music, reading, dancing, hiking, cycling, traveling, and of course, writing poetry and short fiction. Her chapbook, *Dual Exposure,* was published by Blue Light Press in 2015. Her work has appeared in the *Haight Ashbury Literary Journal, Nature Pictures, Poetry Breakfast, River of Earth and Sky: Poems for the Twenty-First Century* and many other anthologies and journals. Barbara lives in Mountain View with her (sane) husband and a (crazy) cat named Kolo.

Deborah Bachels Schmidt: Flutist-turned-poet Deborah Bachels Schmidt has a chapbook forthcoming from Orchard Street Press. Other publication credits include *Blue Unicorn, California Quarterly, The Ekphrastic Review, The Poeming Pigeon,* and *Poetalk.* Never forgetting that she is among the fortunate during this pandemic, she credits introversion, domesticity, and crossword puzzles with getting her through the quarantine. She also takes satisfaction in tracking down runaway ancestors.

Prartho Sereno's prizewinning poetry collections include *Indian Rope Trick, Elephant Raga, Call from Paris,* and *Causing a Stir: The Secret Lives and Loves of Kitchen Utensils.* Poet Laureate Emerita of Marin County California, she has been a Poet in the Schools since 1999 and leads The Poetic Pilgrimage: Poem-Making as Spiritual Practice with adults. During the pandemic, Prartho spent many mornings walking around the lake and afternoons along the backroads of her neighborhood, inspiring her to learn Kate Wolf's "Backroads" on guitar, sing it with abandon, and get back into her studio to paint. One of those paintings made its way onto the cover of this anthology.

Mara Teitel Sheade's poems have appeared in *The Paterson Literary Review, Voices of the Grieving Heart,* and the *Journal of Poetry Therapy,* as well as in several anthologies. She has taught poetry/creative writing in a variety of community settings, including schools, libraries, and Senior Centers. While having done only one jigsaw puzzle during shelter-in-place, she did finally embrace binge watching. The silver lining of shelter-in-place, however, has been being able to participate in writing classes and workshops, consequently generating new work for the first time in a long time!

Betsy Snider is a retired attorney who lives on a lake in rural New Hampshire with the ghosts of her many cats and dogs. She's spent her time in quarantine dreaming of swimming in her lake. She is winner of a 2015 Blue Light Book Award for *Hope is a Muscle.* She was first published in *Lesbian Nuns: Breaking Silence* (Naiad Press, 1985). She has also been published in *The Mud Chronicles; Carrying the Branch; The Lesbian Body; Amore: Love Poems; River of Earth and Sky: Poems for the Twenty-First Century;* and *Love Over 60.* Her new book, *View from the Other Side,* was published in 2020 by Blue Light Press.

Frankie A. Soto is a 2x winner of the Multicultural Poet of the Year award from the National Spoken Word Poetry Awards. The *New York Times* called him an absolute force. He's featured for ABC News, Mayors and has traveled across the country, touring and running workshops at colleges and universities. He tells us, "During this quarantine I've had an opportunity to spend more time with my children, make some killer almond, blueberry, banana pancakes, and focus on finishing my two poetry chapbooks."

Linda Stamps refined the art of talking to herself during the Spring quarantine. Soliloquies led to dialogue and expanded into a chat room of characters, new and old. She managed to write and offer a few poems for publication. Notices of success raised a raucous round of kudos from many of the chat room occupants, except for the naysayers and the bleak-seekers. By the end of the first quarantine, the comedians and absurdists prevailed.

Doreen Stock recently zoom-launched *Tango Man*, a collection of love poems. Other works include: *My Name is Y* (an anti-nuclear memoir); *Three Tales from the Archives of Love* (historical fiction); *In Place of Me* (poems); and *The Politics of Splendor* (poems and translations from the Russian). She is a founding member of The Marin Poetry Center. She does not do puzzles, but during the pandemic has occupied herself with the fine art of literary translation, which draws upon some of the same skills.

Melissa Studdard and **Kelli Russell Agodon** are poets finding connection in quarantine through collaboration. Poems from their series, *The Daily Wave*, have been published in *Seattle Review of Books*, *Berfrois*, the UK's *Inspiration in Isolation*, and Stanford University's *Life in Quarantine: Witnessing Global Pandemic*. Their collaboration was the focus of Catherine Lu's Grammy-nominated PBS/NPR episode "Meet the Queens of Quarantine Poetry." When they Zoom together, they like to wear funny hats.

Steve Trenam: "There are few activities that give me more pleasure than nudging words across the blankly disquieting page, and pushing clay around – into, and through itself. I have been fortunate to work in two disciplines, writing and ceramics, and I have discovered the end result seldom exactly matches the goal. It is the work that matters – the engagement of my imagination, the intuitive use of my mind and hands. I work for Santa Rosa Junior College teaching poetry on Zoom in their Older Adult Program. These classes and my work with Poetic License Sonoma keep me artistically engaged and alive during the Covid 19 pandemic. In my new book, *An Affront to Gravity*, you will find me out on a leafless limb with spider webs and moss, listening to the silken slip of water over stone."

Pat Underwood is author of two chapbooks, *Portraits* and *Gatherings*, a children's book, and a play kit that travels the country. She's a Pushcart nominee and a contributor to *Voices on the Landscape, Contemporary Iowa Poets*. During the pandemic, she has been working on her four acres and writing as much as possible. Her daughter-in-law asked her to write two children's books for their preschool.

Lynn Ungar is a Unitarian Universalist minister, dog trainer and poet who lives in Vancouver, Washington with her two Australian Shepherds. Her book of poetry written during the pandemic times, *These Days*, and a book of earlier poems, *Breathe*, are available at her website, lynnungar.com.

Christine Vovakes' chapbook, *I Didn't Mean to Forget*, won the 2019 Blue Light Poetry Prize. Her poems have appeared in numerous journals and anthologies. *The Washington Post, Sacramento Bee* and *San Francisco Chronicle* have published her articles and photos. She lives in a Northern California rural valley town and tends fruit trees and a large vegetable garden. The erratic schedule of a recently acquired "pandemic puppy" often takes her outside at 3 a.m., where the amazing night sky compensates for sleep deprivation.

Loretta Diane Walker, a musician – tenor saxophonist, a teacher who still likes her students, a breast cancer survivor, an artist who has been humbled and inspired by a collection of remarkable people and poets, is a multiple Pushcart Prize and Best of the Net nominee. She won the 2016 Phillis Wheatley Book Award for Poetry at the Harlem Book Festival, for *In This House*. Loretta is a member of the Texas Institute of Letters. Her debut book, *Word Ghetto* won the 2011 Blue Light Book Award. She teaches elementary music at Reagan Magnet School, Odessa, Texas. Loretta survived the pandemic by juggling reading, writing, word searches, jigsaw puzzles, and watching HGTV with her five-year old nephew. Their favorite show to watch together is Flea Market Flip.

Will Walker lives in San Francisco with his wife and their dog. A former editor of the *Haight Ashbury Literary Journal*, he has two books published by Blue Light Press: *Wednesday after Lunch* and *Zeus at Twilight*. While staying at home, he has gotten acquainted with Zoom technology and has developed exceptional hand-washing skills.

Dorothy Wall is author of *Identity Theory: New and Selected Poems* (Blue Light Press); the essay collection, *Encounters with the Invisible: Unseen Illness, Controversy, and Chronic Fatigue Syndrome*; and coauthor of *Finding Your Writer's Voice: A Guide to Creative Fiction* (St. Martin's Press). Her essays and poems have appeared in numerous magazines and anthologies, and she has taught poetry and fiction writing at San Francisco State University and U.C. Berkeley Extension. She works as a writing coach in Oakland. Since the After Time, her grandson has dyed his hair green, he and his sister have taken up ukulele, and grandma has been their captive audience, from a distance.

George Wallace is writer in residence at the Walt Whitman Birthplace, author of 38 books and chapbooks of poetry, and an editor of Poetrybay and Great Weather for Media, based in NYC. His grandmother, an emigre from Lesbos, Greece, died of the Spanish Flu in NYC in 1919. From mid-March to early July 2020, he stayed strictly in his garden acre in Huntington, Long Island, clearing overgrown land with a hatchet and brush grubber – transplanting saplings and seeding bare patches of lawn with grass.

Florence Weinberger is the author of five books of poetry, the most recent, *Ghost Tattoo*. Along with five nominations for a Pushcart Prize and a nomination for Best of the Net, her poetry has appeared in a long list of literary magazines, including *Spillway, Nimrod, Poetry East, Rattle, Calyx, Miramar, The River Styx, North American Review, The Los Angeles Review*, and *Shenandoah*. Her poems have also been published in many anthologies.

Jasmina Wellinghoff, Ph.D. is a multiple-award winning journalist/editor and a poet. She is currently the editor of ARTS ALIVE SAN ANTONIO and the prose editor of the literary journal VOICES DE LA LUNA. She recently curated a poetry series for ARTS ALIVE SAN ANTONIO, which will soon be published as the anthology, *The Yellow Flag Poems*.

Marsha Whitman has taught music for many years. She continues to enjoy the solace of piano playing, singing and recorder-playing with friends and family online during this time of enforced solitude. Jigsaw puzzles have also been a fun daily activity for Marsha and her husband. Formerly relegated to summer vacations, puzzles have become ever-present. Poetry workshops and continuing to write have lifted her spirits during this pandemic time.

Caryn Leigh Wideman enjoyed pandemic isolation with her husband and puppy, having time for studies, writing, gardening and cleaning out closets. As grief over coronavirus deaths and police brutality cracked her open, she found new friends in Black Lives Matter activists and spiritual healers via social media and Zoom. Her work has appeared in the *San Antonio Express-News, Houston Chronicle, San Antonio Report*, and other publications.

Martin Willitts Jr has decided to hide in a cave, wearing a gas mask during the pandemic. He has made friends with the gopher. He won the *2014 Dylan Thomas International Poetry Contest; Rattle Ekphrastic Challenge*, and has work in *Poetry on The Bus*, which had 48 poems in local buses, including 20 bi-lingual poems from 7 different languages. He has 21 books including *The Temporary World*, which won the 2019 Blue Light Book Award. He is an editor for *The Comstock Review*.

Maw Shein Win's chapbooks are *Ruins of a Glittering Palace* and *Score and Bone. Invisible Gifts: Poems* was published in 2018. She is the first poet laureate of El Cerrito, California (2016 - 2018). Her full-length poetry collection, *Storage Unit for the Spirit House*, was long-listed for the 2021 PEN America Open Book Award and nominated for a Northern California Book Award. She was a Spring 2021 ARC Poetry Fellow at UC Berkeley.

Linda Wing is a poet, teacher, and visual artist who lives in her hometown of Minneapolis, Minnesota. She has been sheltering in place and watching re-runs of nature programs with Ozzy, the cat. Her apartment building is located next door to the bar/restaurant where George Floyd worked as a security guard before the pandemic.

Francine Witte's poetry and fiction have appeared in *Smokelong Quarterly, Wigleaf, Mid-American Review, Passages North*, and many others. Her latest books are *Dressed All Wrong for This* (Blue Light Press), *The*

Way of the Wind, and *The Theory of Flesh.* Her chapbook, *The Cake, The Smoke, The Moon* (flash fiction) is forthcoming from ELJ. She lives in NYC. "During the shelter in place, I worked on my writing, discovered ZOOM readings, and appreciated the quiet."

Joseph Zaccardi: "To write a single poem is a selfless act and a minor miracle. But miracles, minor or otherwise, don't happen by happenstance; they are engendered in part by hard work, in part by the generous help of others, and in part by inspiration and the drive to create. In times of trouble people often turn to poems, and poems often turn into prayers." Joseph Zaccardi is author of *The Weight of Bodily Touches.*

Acknowledgments and Permissions

Malaika King Albrecht: "Praise Song for What Is" and "One Last Drink" were previously published in her book *The Stumble Fields*.

Lucille Lang Day: "Renaming COVID-19" was first published in the *San Francisco Chronicle*. "Pandemic Dream" was first published in *Musings During a Time of Pandemic* (Kistrech Theatre International), edited by Christopher Okemwa.

Johanna Ely: "What I Told Myself" was first published in the *Benicia Herald*.

Diane Frank: "Turtle Island" and "The Genie" are published in *While Listening to the Enigma Variations: New and Selected Poems* (Glass Lyre Press, 2021). "Prayer to the Invisible" was previously published in *Arts Alive San Antonio*, and will be published in *The Yellow Flag Poems*.

Jane Hirshfield: "Today, When I Could Do Nothing" is published here with permission of Jane Hirshfield. It was first published in the Arts and Culture section of the *San Francisco Chronicle*.

Lois P. Jones: "In a Time of Corona" was previously published in *Terrain*. "Camino de Santiago – Journey of the Dead, Day 23, April 2020" was previously published in *21 Fragments: Life in the Time of Covid*.

Ted Kooser: "Pandemic Moon, March, 2020" appears with Ted Kooser's permission as included in *A Suite of Moons*, published by Gibraltar Editions, Omaha (2021).

Dorianne Laux: "Break" was previously published by Carnegie Mellon Press, and published here with permission of Dorianne Laux. "Joy" and "In any Event" are published here with permission of Dorianne Laux.

Carey Link: "A House of Bones" was first published in her chapbook, *To Light a House of Bones* (Blue Light Press, 2021).

Emilie Lygren: "Substitutions for Buttermilk" was previously published in *What We Were Born For* (Blue Light Press, 2021) and in the literary journal *Index for the Next World*.

Megan Merchant: "A House of Manifestos" was previously published in *Bracken* magazine.

Claudine Nash: "Permission Slip" was previously published in *Peeking Cat Poetry.* "Looking up after the Storm" was previously published in *Hibiscus.*

Barbara Quick: "In the Before Times" was first published in the *San Francisco Chronicle.* "Pandemic Pumpkins" was published in the 2021 *Farmer-ish Print Annual.*

Mary Kay Rummel: "A Turn Toward Red," "For All That Is Lost," and "In a Time of Distancing" were previously published in *Nocturnes: Between Flesh and Stone* (Blue Light Press, 2021).

Betsy Snider: "Stones for the Dead" was previously published in *View from the Other Side* (Blue Light Press, 2020).

Maw Shein Win: "Winter Hair" was previously published in *The Banyan Review* (Winter 2020).

Francine Witte: "We live now" was previously published in *unbroken journal,* Issue 28, January 2021.

CPSIA information can be obtained
at www.ICGtesting.com
Printed in the USA
LVHW010224121121
702939LV00002B/37